Reading in the Dark

Reading in the Dark

Using Film as a Tool in the English Classroom

John Golden
Grant High School
Portland, Oregon

National Council of Teachers of English
1111 W. Kenyon Road, Urbana, Illinois 61801-1096

Staff Editor: Tom Tiller

Interior Design: Doug Burnett

Cover Design: Diana Coe

Digital Imagery ©2001 PhotoDisc, Inc.

NCTE Stock Number: 38721-3050

Film photos: Museum of Modern Art/Film Stills Archive. Courtesy of Colum-
bia Pictures (*The Remains of the Day*), MGM (*North by Northwest*), Miramax Films
(*Life Is Beautiful*), Paramount Pictures (*The Conversation, Rear Window,* and *Vertigo*), RKO Pictures (*Citizen Kane* and *Notorious*), The Samuel Goldwyn Company (*Henry V*), Twentieth Century Fox (*Edward Scissorhands*), United Artists
(*Othello* and *Rocky*), Universal City Studios (*Do the Right Thing*), Universal Pictures (*Crooklyn, Frankenstein,* and *Psycho*), and Warner Bros. (*The Color Purple*).

Library of Congress Cataloging-in-Publication Data

Golden, John, 1968–
        Reading in the dark : using film as a tool in the English classroom/John Golden.
             p. cm.
        Includes bibliographical references.
        ISBN 0-8141-3872-1 (pbk.)
         1. Language arts (Middle school) 2. Motion pictures in education. I. Title.
     LB1631 .G619 2001
     428.4—dc21

                                                                                          2001042754

For Laura, who honestly believes that anything is possible and who started me on this by asking, "Why not?"

And for Eleanor, who arrived just in time to be included here, and to spit up at least once on the manuscript.

Contents

Figures

Acknowledgments

If the actual writing of this book was a lonely exercise, the learning, background, and assistance I needed to complete it involved a lot of dedicated and talented educators, family members, friends, and students who guided, directed, taught, and encouraged me.

First of all, some folks at the College Board—Lola Greene, Steve Green, and Trisha Callender—gave me a number of opportunities to present and develop many of these activities with their support and guidance.

The real genesis of this project was a conversation—or argument, depending on whose version you hear—with Bill McBride of Colorado State University about a film project in the Pacesetter program. To anyone who knows him, Bill is a champion for teachers and their ideas. And since I let him win that argument, he introduced me to Pete Feely, of NCTE, who actually thought we could try the ideas out as a book and who has shown patience beyond any reasonable expectation. Tom Tiller, an editor at NCTE, improved this project immeasurably with every suggestion he made. He did such a wonderful job that I will be sending him all my students' essays to edit from now on.

Thanks to Gary Cowan of Nashville Public Schools, Jenny Oren Krugman of Miami-Dade Public Schools, Karen Kerlin of Fulton County (Georgia) Schools, Rojulene Norris of Prince George's County (Maryland) Schools, and Linda Christensen of Portland Public Schools for letting me practice and refine many of these strategies in presentations to their teachers. To Gary, a special note of thanks for recognizing something in these strategies long before I did and for helping me to define the structure of this book to fit what teachers really need.

Though I've always had an interest in film, Cynthia Lucia of New York University and Enie Vaisburd of the Northwest Film Center gave me the concepts and tools to be able to talk about it. Much of what I have written here came from their wonderfully engaging classes.

Teachers are sponges, and I soaked up many great ideas from other educators that found their way into this book. Thank you to David Whitley, formerly of Nashville Public Schools, Ann Foster of Brevard County (Florida) Schools, Karen Nulton of the Educational Testing Service, Jo Ellen Victoreen of San Jose Unified District, Betsy James of the College Board, Flora Levin and Robin Knapp of Fulton County (Georgia) Schools, and David Quinn of Edmonds Woodbury High School in Washington.

Thanks to my folks, Dick and Chris Golden, for giving me the tools, and to my sisters, Julie French and Kathy Darby, who always encouraged me and made me feel that I was able to do something like this.

Thanks so much to my colleagues in Maryland—Tracy Gray, Maura Kelly, and Pat Brooks—and to my colleagues in Portland—Kevin Cline, Alex Gordin, Jim Mayer, Vina Schaeffer, and Toni Hunter.

Thanks, of course, to my students from Bowie High School and Grant High School, who not only—unwittingly—allowed me to use them as guinea pigs, but who also were very patient during my short-tempered writing months when their essays took a long, long time to return. A special thank you to Ariela Edelman for taking pictures for the project.

And a final acknowledgment to Laura Lull, who reads film with such a fine eye and with her whole heart, and who improved this project and clarified my thinking in more ways than I can name.

Introduction

"It's Movie Day!"

Lights go off, heads go down, and teachers finally get some grading done.

Using film in the classroom is better than this, of course, but every time I wheel that VCR down the hallway, I know what the other teachers—and my principal—are thinking: "Is Golden showing another movie? Doesn't he teach at all?" All right, maybe they don't think that; maybe I only *think* they think that, which is just as bad. Why do we still feel somewhat guilty about showing a film in school? Maybe because everyone in the school knows about that one teacher who shows all the *Star Trek* films to his classes three times a year.

But what really happens when we show movies in the English classroom? Oftentimes, what we show is the film version of a written text that our students have read or are in the midst of reading, or an extension of a written text that might have similar characters, time periods, or themes. In addition, some teachers are fortunate enough to be able to teach film history or film as its own separate and unique text.

There are several books that address each of these uses of film, and I refer to these books in Appendix A (Resources), but what I hope this project proposes is a way to use film even more actively by incorporating it into our traditional ways of teaching reading and literature. Even though this book deals with cinematic technique and film study, it is ultimately a book about using film to help students improve their reading and analytical skills.

Kids tend to be visually oriented, able to point out every significant image in a three-minute MTV music video, but when it comes to doing the same with a written text, they stare at it as if they are reading German. Nonetheless, we know, or strongly suspect, that the skills they use to decode the visual image are the same skills they use for a written text, and our goal, therefore, is to use that immediate interest in and uncanny ability with film and to make it work for us. What this guide does, then, is suggest skills that your students might want to practice by responding to film clips and then—hopefully—transfer to written texts.

I first became aware of these additional possibilities for film when I was teaching a senior-level English class that included a five-week unit on the study of film. We discussed the cinematic aspects of several films, including such things as sound, lighting, and editing; the students enjoyed it and learned a good deal about motion pictures, though most students complained that they could never just watch a movie anymore: they would, unconsciously at least, analyze it. I laughed and said "sorry," but what I really noticed was that when we turned to a novel in the next unit, my students seemed to be much more willing to critique and analyze that written work than they had been before the film unit. On the next year's guinea pigs, I tested this theory further by moving that unit up earlier into our school year. I discovered that it was not just students' analytical skills that improved: it was also their reading skills. Now, they didn't know that, and I certainly didn't tell them, but it was true: the watching and analyzing of movies seemed to greatly affect their ability to read and critique literature.

So, as my colleague Gary Cowan recently put it, maybe we have been going about using film in the wrong order. We tend to read a written text and then watch its counterpart on film, but what this book is suggesting is that we reverse the order: use a film clip to practice the reading and analytical skills that we want our students to have and *then* turn to the written text.

Another colleague, Kevin Cline, described these strategies as just another weapon for teachers to be able to pull out of their arsenals, or another rabbit from their bags of tricks, if you prefer a less combative metaphor. Film, then, can be used in the same way that minilessons on grammar, readers workshop, and vocabulary practice can be woven in and out of our teaching. In turn, I hope this book will be a source for activities that you can slip in and out of your regular curriculum (and there is just so much time for "slipping in" extra things, isn't there?) whenever you identify certain skills that your students lack in reading and/or critical analysis.

As an English teacher, you will not need any great background or experience in teaching film in order to use this guide. Many excellent texts referred to throughout and highlighted in Appendix A do a much more thorough job of introducing film history, theory, and criticism, but this book will try to get you started tomorrow, or maybe the day after. Chapter 1 is an introduction to some basic film terminology that will give you and your students the language—and the confidence—to talk about film. Chapter 2 then suggests several reading strategies, such as predicting, responding, and questioning, that can be practiced with film, and Chapter 3 continues this approach by practicing literary analysis with film clips, addressing topics such as characterization, setting, and irony.

Too often, curriculum developers, district supervisors, and building administrators are reluctant to encourage the use of film because they think that the only way to use it in the classroom is to show the entire movie, which can take three to four class periods. I rarely show entire films unless it is part of a film unit; rather, I suggest using short clips from movies, some as short as two minutes and none longer than fifteen, that highlight the skill you are trying to practice with your students.

If you are interested in teaching complete films, however, Chapter 4 suggests several movies with grade-level recommendations, possible time frames, and discussion questions. This section maintains the same emphasis on the desire to improve our students' reading and analytical skills even as they watch movies.

Each of the films referred to in this guide is widely available in most video rental stores and should be appropriate for high school and middle school classes, though of course you will want to preview each before using it in class to determine its appropriateness to your local district. Most of the clips come from films that are rated "PG-13" or lower, though some do have an "R" rating, and I identify these at the beginning of the clip's analysis. Only one of the clips suggested here contains any vulgarity (the "s" word, once), and none contain nudity or excessive violence, though the film as a whole may, so, again, please preview and use your local guidelines to assist you.

You'll also notice that most of the films are popular or at least fairly well known; there are few foreign films and no real "art films" or obscure classic movies. This is not to say that those films would not work as well or better, but only that I like to show my students films that come fairly easily to them in terms of recognizing the actors, the directors, or even the movie itself.

As you read through descriptions of these clips and complete films, I am sure that you're going to be thinking about your favorite movies, and you will say, "Hey, I know a movie that would work for this!" which is exactly what should happen. These are films that I liked first and then thought about using in the classroom. I say: If you like it, and it works, use it.

The counter information refers to the hour, minute, and second as your VCR counter would count from the very first image that appears on the screen after all of the previews, advertisements, copyright warnings, and rating information. So, when you get to that place, reset your counter to zero and fast-forward to the time listed for the clip. Because

VCR counters may vary, I tried to describe the scene in enough detail that you will be able to find it easily.

Good luck, and remember: Every time you wheel that VCR down the hallway to try out one of these activities, put out the lights and feel good about it, but please don't tell them I suggested it—I get into enough trouble on my own.

1 Film Terminology and Cinematic Effects

As English teachers, we feel comfortable discussing the important elements of a poem, short story, or novel because we have had practice and background in discussing the effect that, say, word choice, meter, imagery, or point of view is supposed to have on the reader. We know that a poet using a particular rhyme scheme or metaphor is no doubt doing it on purpose, and we are able to guide our students to recognize the craft of the writer in doing so. Like the poet, a filmmaker uses various devices and techniques for a desired effect.

When a director uses a particular lighting choice or camera angle, for example, he or she may be trying to say something about the character or situation. It is this fine attention to the craft of the director that will assist us later in applying critical analysis to the craft of the writer of a print text. To that end, this chapter is an attempt to make you feel as comfortable with discussing film as you are with discussing literature. Oftentimes, we feel at a disadvantage in teaching film because we think that our students may know more than we do. But this brief introduction will give you the vocabulary and the examples you need in order to feel confident.

As a way to introduce several key film techniques, my colleague David Whitley would roll up a piece of paper, call it a camera, and use it as a way to help students visualize the various cinematic shots and angles. When students look through the rolled-up paper, they pretend that they are looking through the lens of a movie camera. Sure, it's cheesy, but it works, and if you're like most public school teachers, you probably don't have thirty-five cameras just sitting around. (See Figure 1 to find out how cheesy it looks.)

Throughout this chapter, cinematic techniques are illustrated through inclusion of movie stills as well as photographs taken specifically for this book, and at the end of the chapter I discuss several short film clips that can be used in your classroom to introduce the techniques and illustrate their effects on viewers.

The Shot

This is the building block of all filmmaking. Whenever you hear someone say, "Hey, did you see that shot in *The Godfather*?" he or she is talking

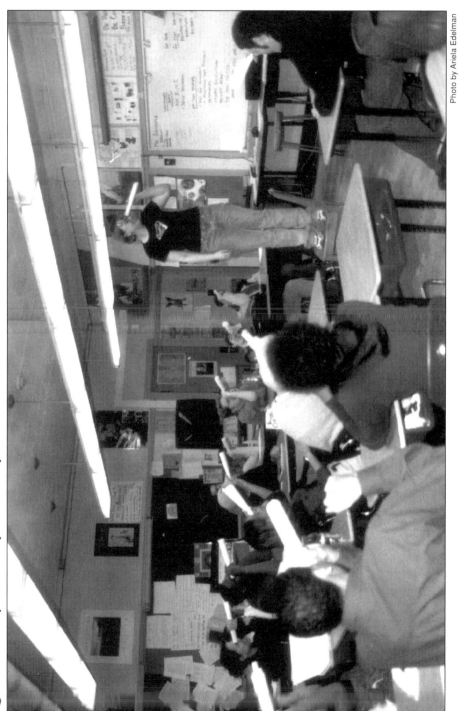

Figure 1. This is just how they do it in Hollywood.

about a single, uninterrupted piece of film. In other words, the shot is the image that is seen on-screen until it is replaced by another image through some type of editing technique (see discussion later in this chapter).

As you look through your paper camera, blink for just a second; this is the same quick "cut" between shots in a film. If the camera moves while still filming, but without that momentary break, then you are still watching just the one shot. Play a clip from any film and you'll see that moment of black when the shot changes. While the black is not actually inserted into the film, it seems to be there for just a split second. As you watch a clip in class, play it without sound and have students clap or snap their fingers every time a new shot appears. They'll pick it up quickly.

Framing

One of the first decisions that a director has to make is how the object will be positioned within the shot, or how much of the frame of the movie screen the object will occupy. The three main framing types are the long shot, the close-up, and the medium shot. As we will see, a director will choose to use a given type of shot in order to achieve a particular effect.

Long Shot

Have your students take their rolled-up "cameras" and look at you so that they see your entire body. You may need to stand in the far corner of your room. They are framing you in a long shot. In a long shot, the object on the screen appears small or appears to be seen from some distance away. If a person is shown, then generally you will see his or her entire body. This type of shot can establish the scene, by showing, say, the Manhattan skyline, so that the viewer knows where the film will take place. It can also serve to show distance or separation between characters in a way that other shots cannot, or to show that a character is integrated with his or her surroundings—as in Figure 2, which shows the blues singer Shug surrounded by her admiring fans in *The Color Purple*—or somehow at odds with them because the background becomes as large and important within the frame as the character is. The long shot gives the viewer a sense of time and place, but objects and characters may seem unclear or indistinct because of the distance and lack of detail. It also allows the viewer to decide where to look since there is so much on the screen to see. The long shot—in many ways—can be seen as the opposite of the next framing choice, the close-up.

Figure 2. This is a perfect reason to use a long shot: imagine what you would miss if this shot from *The Color Purple* were a medium or close shot. The long shot allows the viewer to see that Shug is the center of it all.

Close-up or Close Shot

Have your students look back at you through their "cameras" and have them roll them up more tightly so that only your face can be seen through the hole. Now have them look only at a coffee cup that you are holding in your hand (during first period, I'm sure there's one glued to your hand!). This is called a close-up or close shot. The object or subject takes up nearly 80 percent of the screen space and therefore appears to be very large. This shot can be used by a filmmaker to direct the viewer's attention to a crucial clue in a detective story, to emphasize a facial expression or gesture, or, perhaps, to show the single tear dropping off the character's cheek as he delivers his deathbed speech. The close-up forces the viewer to look at only what the director intended, as opposed to the long shot, which allows for at least some choice on the part of the viewer. Interesting, too, with a close-up is what is missing, or excluded from the scene. We are not allowed to see the entire scene, so we become deprived for a time of the overall context. The close-up is uniquely cinematic—theatergoers, in contrast, are not allowed up onstage to see the sly wink or the trembling hands—but, as we will see later, the close-up has many parallels in literature. It is one of the most powerful tools a filmmaker has: it is intimate and revealing, though somewhat intrusive and authoritative.

Medium Shot

Still looking at you through their paper cameras, your students should now unroll them a bit until they can see you from about the waist up. This type of shot is called a medium shot (between a long and a close shot) and is probably the most common and most naturalistic of the three types, since it is also the most common in our real lives. Generally we see each other in medium shots because of personal space distances. Unlike the long and close shots, the medium shot does not necessarily communicate much in the way of cinematic effect, and it could best be called a sort of "neutral shot." Most television shows are framed almost entirely by using medium shots because they are unobtrusive and comfortable; they do not tend to call attention to themselves. I've never heard any of my students say, "Wow! What a great medium shot, man!" Not to disrespect the shot entirely—the medium shot can show more setting and context than a close-up can, though it lacks the close-up's detail, and it brings the viewer closer to the subject than the long shot does, though it cannot show the distance and relationships between characters, or between characters and settings, in quite the same way.

There are almost unlimited variations on these framing choices. There is an extreme close-up, a three-quarter medium shot, and a "deep-focus shot," where, in a single shot, one object is shown in a close-up while others in the background are shown in a long shot. (See Figure 3 for an example from *Citizen Kane* where deep focus is used to show the distance between characters.) So, as with all the cinematic techniques we will be seeing, the fun involves decoding the director's intentions and supporting one's judgment with specific details. Classic Hollywood framing normally suggests that a director establish the scene with a long shot, move into a medium shot, and only then use a close-up. This has a natural kind of feel to it: as an audience member you can imagine getting closer and closer to the subject. Interesting things occur, however, when a director intentionally breaks with this convention for whatever ideas that he or she may have.

Focus

Now obviously, when we think of focus, we really just want to say to the director, "Yes, please put it into focus for us, thanks." But there are ways for a director to play with the focus in order to communicate something to the audience.

Soft Focus

When we look at family pictures from the Grand Canyon, there is always at least one that is ruined by being out of focus. But to filmmakers, there are varying degrees of focus. Without giving the audience a headache, a director can film his or her subject just ever-so-slightly out of focus, which creates a texture called soft focus. Classic Hollywood actresses used to insist on this type of focus for their close-ups. Today, it is common to see soft focus in romantic films to help create a lighter mood, but it can also be used to blur an image slightly in order to communicate uncertainty. Many scenes with the Madeleine/Judy character in Hitchcock's *Vertigo* are shot with a soft focus since her identity and motives are always in question. In contrast, directors may wish to film their subjects in sharp focus, which distinguishes the image in brilliant clarity. Movies that are trying for a high degree of realism might employ sharp focus, though it is not as easy to recognize as is soft focus.

Rack Focus

Imagine a scene from a film where the character is in focus in the background of the shot. He is nervous and pacing. Suddenly the phone rings.

Figure 3. Orson Welles often used deep focus in *Citizen Kane* to show the distance between characters, as in this shot that speaks volumes about the lack of intimacy between Kane and his wife.

The character goes out of focus and the phone in the foreground is now in focus. We know this call is important. The director of this silly scene used rack focus to force viewers to direct their attention where he or she wanted them to look. A director can use this technique to bring either the background or the foreground suddenly into focus. Contemporary filmmaker Michael Mann uses rack focus in many of his films, such as *Heat* and *The Insider,* as a way to show the changing power and relationships that can occur within a single scene, but without having to cut from his shot. If not overused, rack focus is a very effective way of combining the languid pace of a continuous take (see "editing" below) with the power of a close-up that directs the audience's attention.

Deep Focus

Some filmmakers—Orson Welles and William Wyler among them—championed the use of deep focus photography, which allows for all objects in the foreground as well as in the background to remain in focus. *Citizen Kane* is a textbook example of using deep focus, often to show relationships between characters and objects in their environment. (Refer back to Figure 3 for the shot showing distance between Kane and his wife, both of whom are in focus.) Some critics argue that deep focus gives a greater sense of reality, since in real life we can choose what to look at; we are not often forced in and out of focus, and I rarely see anyone but my wife in a close-up. Welles himself said that "the public may choose, with its eyes, what it wants to see in a shot. I don't like to force it" (Giannetti 1999). Even if it is not more realistic than normal focus, a director using the deep focus concept can literally fill his or her frame with information and create interesting compositions.

Angles

Another consideration that the director must take into account is where the camera will be placed in relation to the subject. He or she may choose to use a low, high, eye-level, or Dutch angle.

Low Angle

Have your students, seated at their desks, take their rolled-up paper cameras and look up at you standing in, say, a medium shot. It would be even more dramatic if you were to stand up on a chair or a desk. (Author's note: I'm pretty sure that I cannot be held liable for any injury you might sustain from trying to demonstrate any of these techniques, especially the dolly shot described below, but be careful anyway, or, even better, have a student do it—they're more expendable and less likely to sue.) When the students look at you, the camera is *below* the subject and we have what's called a low-angle shot. How do you look when viewed through that camera below you? Just as you always want to appear to your students: huge, powerful, dominating, and in control. Characters shot with a low angle are often the more powerful ones in the film. (See Figure 4 for an example showing Othello as a menacing character.) Size and strength can be exaggerated and commented on by the use of the low angle, which will become a very important factor when we look at characterization later on.

High Angle

Now, it's your turn. Standing—on a chair or otherwise—take your "camera" and look down at your students. This time the camera is above the subject in what is called a high-angle shot. And how do your students look to you now? Small, weak, powerless, trapped? Not unlike a normal class period, then? Characters presented with a high-angle shot in film are the ones who appear a little weaker and less in control. A great scene that you might recall comes from the beginning of *North by Northwest* when Cary Grant runs out of the United Nations Building after being falsely accused of murder. The camera is way, way above him as he runs away, tiny and weak, as the forces of the conspiracy tower over him. In fact, you may have to look at the scene twice; he looks so small, you can easily miss him. Or consider Figure 5, showing a high-angle shot of James Stewart in Hitchcock's *Vertigo*.

Eye Level

If you sit down with your students and have them look at you and at each other through their cameras, you are now seeing each other at eye level. Obviously this is a shot, like the medium shot above, that carries no immediate, readily apparent significance on its own, and it can best be considered another sort of "neutral shot." Characters are on an even balance with this type of angle. That said, however, if a director uses an eye-level shot of a character after setting him or her up with a series of high-angle shots, the director may be commenting on the growing strength or confidence of this character.

Dutch Angle

Have your students take their cameras, and look at you in a close-up, but, as they do so, go ahead and kind of lean a bit to one side. Within

Figure 4. Excellent use of the low angle emphasizes Othello's power (in Orson Welles's
Othello)

Figure 5. The camera above the James Stewart character not only emphasizes his weakness in *Vertigo* but also shows the precarious situation in which he has found himself.

their frame, you look a little off-kilter. To create a real Dutch or "canted" angle, the camera itself tilts slightly, but the effect is the same. The image appears sideways, to one extent or another, within the frame. This type of angle is often used in horror or gangster films to show an evil character or a dangerous situation. A Dutch angle can create tension or peculiarity in an otherwise static or normal situation, thus implying danger or moral uncertainty. The climactic scene in Spike Lee's *Do The Right Thing*, for example, uses several Dutch angles, coupled with extreme close-ups of two characters whose argument and subsequent fight turn the neighborhood into a riot. The use of the Dutch angle lets us know that all is not well and the situation will soon explode.

Camera Movement

Many of the earliest films were short documents of daily life: people going into a factory, a blacksmith's shop, and, to the reported shrieks of the audience—unused to the perspective—a train pulling into a station. These images were captured by an immobile camera fixed upon a tripod, but camera operators quickly designed ways for the camera to move, or appear to move, in order to keep getting those audience shrieks.

Pan

Have your students look at you through their "cameras" in a long shot as you walk back and forth at the front of the classroom. The cameras are not technically moving since the students have not—hopefully—left their seats and thus only their heads pivoted in order to follow the action. When the camera pivots along the horizontal axis like this, the movement is called a pan, which is often used in film to introduce the setting. As Bernard Dick points out in his excellent *Anatomy of Film*, this movement in film often goes left to right because for Western readers/viewers this is most natural, but it is not absolute (1998, 48). The opening of Hitchcock's *Rear Window*, for example, is made up of a series of right-to-left pans that show the courtyard where the entire film will take place and where most of the relevant characters live. A pan is also often used from the point of view of characters as they take in their surroundings or situations. Think how often you have seen characters in a horror film, for example, look around in the old, decaying mansion in which they have found themselves, and the camera pans around to reveal the source of their fear.

Tilt

Like you did for the low angle, you may want a student—or your stunt double—to stand in for you for this one. Have students look at you in a medium shot as you step back onto your desk or a chair and then back down again. In order to keep you in their frame this time, your students had to move their heads up and down—thus, in effect, tilting—along the vertical axis. Technically, as with the pan, the camera did not move—only the camera's head moved. The tilt is an extremely effective way to communicate distance, size, and strength. Imagine a film where a character is preparing to climb the sheer rock face of a mountain. We see her from behind as she looks up, and then we tilt up, keep tilting, and keep tilting until far in the distance we see the mountain's top. The audience now knows what this climber will attempt. Another great use of a tilt is to show power. In *Citizen Kane,* the young Charles Kane has been given a sled by his guardian, whose voice we hear off-screen, but only the lower half of his body is visible. The camera catches the boy looking up and then tilts up for quite awhile until it finally reveals the face looking down upon the child. (See Figure 6 for an example from *The Conversation.*) The tilt also has quite a history of being part of the objective male gaze toward female sexuality. Think how often you have seen a film in which the camera, following a man's gaze, focuses on the leg or foot of a woman and then slowly tilts up to reveal the rest of the woman.

Zoom

This is the trickiest of all your paper camera operations, and it really taxes the limits of our technology. Have your students look at you in long shot, but then, without taking the camera away, they should try to slowly roll the camera up tighter until they have you framed in a medium shot. Again, as with the pan and tilt, there was no real movement, but in this case, the tightening of the paper made you—the object—appear to grow in size within the frame. This is similar to what happens when a camera zooms: the focal length of the lens changes, thus making the object appear to move closer or further away. The zoom is a way to direct the audience's attention to a detail that the director does not want us to miss. We move into the scene without leaving our seats.

Tracking or Dolly Shots

Once your "victim" has signed all proper release forms, have the student volunteer, with his or her camera, sit in a chair with wheels. (If you

Figure 6. Dramatizing an individual's plight in the face of enormous institutional power, the low-angle shot captured in this publicity still for *The Conversation* would quite possibly have been a tilt as well if Francis Ford Coppola hadn't decided to leave it on the cutting-room floor.

do not have one with wheels, have two or three of your strongest students sign more release papers and have them pick up the volunteer—chair and all.) Walk around the classroom as the student films you, but this time the student should be pushed—or carried—as he or she films. Now, for the first time, we have true movement of the camera itself. Any time that the camera is moving like this, the shot is called a tracking or dolly shot. This is by far the most uniquely cinematic of all these movements since it can enter and actually move us through the imaginative space of the film in the way that the pan and tilt cannot because they are stationary movements, more reminiscent of watching a staged play. We can now go with the action, become part of it, or even go behind it, instead of merely watching as it passes us by. The camera may be on a track, a truck, or a helicopter, or it may even be held in the operator's hands—all of which can be referred to as a dolly shot or as tracking. Though there are several types of tracking movements with specific names, they do not really concern us here, but if you have an interest be sure to look in the resource summary in Appendix C for the texts on filmmaking. Oftentimes it may be difficult to distinguish if a camera is zooming in on an object or whether it is dollying in. One way to tell is to look at the background to see if it changes in relation to the objects and flattens a bit, which means you have a zoom. The other way is to ignore it and just enjoy the movie. (This last piece of advice was given to me by my fourth-period class after just such a debate, though I believe an expletive was used.)

Lighting

If you can trade your paper cameras for a flashlight or two, then we can examine the essential role that lighting can play in creating a particular effect desired by the director. The principal source of light on a movie set is called the "key light," and other lights balance, soften, and shade the key light. Two general descriptors of film lighting are "low-key lighting" and "high-key lighting," terms which are used to characterize the lighting of an overall scene. Two others—"side/bottom lighting" and "front lighting"—are used primarily on actors and actresses to editorialize on some aspect of their characters.

Low-Key Lighting

Turn off all the lights in the classroom, but leave maybe just your overhead projector and a flashlight on. As students look around, they will see an example of a scene that could be called "low-key." Its chief characteristics are its darkness, shadows, and patches of bright key light, provided in this case by the overhead projector and the flashlight. Obviously, low-key lighting can create moods of suspicion, mystery, and danger. This type of lighting is great for horror films, film noir, and detective movies, because things can be hidden or concealed in the depth of shadows.

High-Key Lighting

Switch your classroom lights on again, and open up all the blinds and curtains. As students look around now, they are looking at high-key lighting, unless, like my students, they are in Portland, Oregon, where, during the winter, there is no such thing as high-key light anywhere. This type of lighting is distinguished by its brightness, openness, and lack of shadows or contrasts between light and dark. Your romantic comedies, musicals, and costumed dramas are often filmed with high-key lighting, since, with this type of lighting, characters and situations are seen without misunderstanding or threat.

Neutral Lighting

Not every scene *must* be either high- or low-key; a scene could be sort of average, or lacking in much to distinguish its lighting. When the lighting is even and balanced throughout the shot, it might best be described as "neutral." Most television programs are shot with this type of evenness in mind. Notice a trend going? A medium shot with an eye-level angle and neutral lighting might not be saying too much, though we know at least what it might *not* be saying.

Bottom/Side Lighting

Go ahead and return your classroom to that "low-key" effect again. Now take your flashlight and shine it about two inches underneath your chin, pointing upward. This is the same thing you did when you told ghost stories around the campfire. How do you look? Well, I don't know how you looked before, but now the light illuminates only parts of your face, and the shadows distort it so you look a little scary. Take a volunteer and shine your flashlight on the side of his or her face, so that only one eye or the mouth receives any light. This type of lighting—bottom or side lighting—has the effect of creating characters that may be evil, are hiding something, are morally ambiguous, or are conflicted in some way.

Front Lighting

Getting another volunteer from your class, shine your flashlight evenly across the subject's face, so that no shadows appear; you have created the effect of front lighting. Look at the volunteer's hair: it probably takes on a bit of a "halo effect." This type of lighting is often used to show innocence or openness, and was considered absolutely essential for most Hollywood actresses. A character who is honest with nothing to hide will often be shot this way—the hero or heroine in particular.

Some of the most striking examples of these lighting choices come from black-and-white films (see, for example, the shot from *Othello* in Figure 7). The contrast between light and dark is just not as readily apparent in color film, though each of these lighting decisions, and the implications behind them, are still in use in today's films. Because the way in which characters and scenes are lit can give an audience so much information so quickly—and often without dialogue—lighting is one of the most important tools that filmmakers have at their disposal with which to assist the viewer in understanding characters, setting, tone, and theme. Ruth Warrick, who starred in *Citizen Kane,* said in the documentary *Reflections on Citizen Kane* (1991) that director Orson Welles wanted viewers to understand everything about the characters and the situations through the lighting and the camera angles. Look at any random scene from that movie and see how successful Welles was.

Sound

Sound is often overlooked (really, no pun intended) in the study of film, though it is probably equally as important as the visual image is in its ability to create an effect on a viewer. A violin can make us feel sad during the deathbed speech, a gunshot can make us jump out of our seats, and a voice-over narration can help us follow the story, though we rarely comment on the "really awesome sound in that movie." There are many ways to classify sound in film—dialogue, music, sound effects—and there are various ways to analyze the sound in a film—pitch, timbre, direction, whether it's on-screen or off-screen—but the categories that are most important in their application to literature are these: diegetic, nondiegetic, and internal diegetic.

Diegetic Sound

This is a confusing-sounding term for an easy concept. Any sound that could logically be heard by a character within the movie environment is called diegetic sound, pronounced "dī-uh-je-tik." If a character speaks or coughs, or a cat growls, this is diegetic sound. Typical diegetic sounds include such things as background noise, traffic, dialogue between characters, and the like. The important distinction to make is that the audi-

Figure 7. This is a perfect example from *Othello* of varied lighting within the same shot, with Othello in darkness and Desdemona brightly lit.

ence and the characters hear roughly the same thing. Or, at least, the characters *could* have heard the sounds the audience heard.

Nondiegetic Sound

Imagine that you are a character in the movie *Jaws*. You're just swimming in the middle of the night in shark-infested waters, minding your own business when you hear "duh-duhn . . . duh-duhn." Now, of course you would get out of the water quickly because you know a big fish is on its way. But why don't those stupid characters in the film do the same? Actually, they're probably not that stupid; it's because the sound is "nondiegetic"—that is, sound that cannot be heard logically by characters within the film. Any sound that is intended *only* for the audience and is not a part of the environment of the film is called nondiegetic. Oftentimes this means music (but remember, music can also be within the film if the characters are listening to it), but it can also take the form of voice-over narration. When the voice-over is saying something, you don't usually hear a character in the film respond to or correct the narrator, because, again, this is nondiegetic, though there are some exceptions to these classifications of sound (see below).

Internal Diegetic Sound

What if a character is talking to himself? Or what if a character is remembering sounds she heard before? If only the one character can hear these things, the sound can be called internal diegetic, since presumably it is logical that the character hearing them *can* hear them, whereas other characters do not (and perhaps *could* not logically) hear them. This distinction could be called a mix of the two other sound types, but it is an important definition to have when thinking about narration and point of view in literature.

What's the point in making these three distinctions between types of sound? Sometimes the director—like a writer—wants to give information or clues directly to his or her audience without giving that same information to the characters, and it is important to be able to know when and how the director is doing this. Oftentimes, through the varying use of diegetic and nondiegetic sound, the director can create suspense, irony, or foreshadowing. Directors also play with these distinctions for other reasons. Mel Brooks, in his Western parody *Blazing Saddles*, shows a group of cowboys riding up a hill to the sounds of a swelling orchestral piece, but when they get to the top, they (and the audience) see that there is, in fact, an orchestra playing right there in the middle of nowhere. The opening of *The Magnificent Ambersons* by

Orson Welles includes a voice-over that is seemingly spoken by a third-person omniscient narrator, until you realize that the townspeople are finishing his sentences and picking up where he left off. The sound in the film acts as a sort of Greek chorus to catch the audience up with the story. Francis Ford Coppola's *The Conversation* is all about a man trying to reconstruct the meaning behind one (seemingly) innocent conversation that he recorded between two people, but along the way the dialogue continues to move back and forth between diegetic, nondiegetic, and even internal diegetic. The result of these sound manipulations is an exploration of the nature of privacy and obsession.

Editing

So far, the cinematic techniques that we have been discussing have boiled down to what the director decides to put into his or her frame or onto the soundtrack. The angle, the lighting, the focus, and the sound are parts of that shot, but how do shots get put together? That's editing. In its simplest terms, editing refers to the methods by which a director chooses to move from one shot to another. The most common type of edit is called a "cut," which is what we saw earlier when we were defining a shot: Quite literally, one piece of film is cut and then affixed to another piece, and the result is that tiny, split second of black (like a blink) before the next shot appears. This is far and away the most common and the quickest method of editing two or more shots together, but it is hardly the only type available to a director or editor. Others include the fade, the dissolve, the crosscut, the flashback, and the eye-line match.

The Fade

This type of edit occurs when the image on-screen slowly fades away and the screen itself is entirely black (or some other color) for a noticeable period of time, and then a new image slowly fades in from that black screen. Directors like to use the fade to denote the end of a scene, as an author might do by ending the chapter, perhaps, but it can also be used within the same scene to show that some measure of time has passed. We probably remember this technique most from the old movies when the man and woman would go into the bedroom, the image would fade out, and then it would fade in on the two of them smoking cigarettes. The inference is clear: time has passed and something (?!?) has happened. The fade tends to be a very slow type of transition and not a particularly realistic effect (when was the last time that you saw someone fade out in front of you?), so its use is usually carefully chosen.

The Dissolve

As with the fade, the image slowly begins to fade out, but instead of fading all the way to black, it is replaced by another image that is slowly fading in. The dissolve is a slow transition, too, and because two images are on-screen at the same time, its effect cannot be underestimated. The dissolve is often used as a way to make a connection between two objects or characters that the viewer might not have made without its use. Think, for example, of the next-to-last-shot in *Psycho*. We see Norman's face slowly dissolving into the skeleton face of his mother: the two are one again. Or think about the use of the dissolve in James Cameron's *Titanic*. The director shows the audience several shots of the ship as it currently appears on the ocean floor, and then dissolves into shots of the ocean liner in the past in all its shining glory. The effect is for the audience to see and feel the narrator bringing this tale and the boat back to life for us.

The Crosscut

Picture this: The scene is a quiet, suburban town, where children are playing in the front yards. The director cuts from this scene immediately to a shot of a missile screaming across the sky. Then another cut back to the town, and once more back to the missile. The audience knows exactly what is happening: that missile is coming to this town. This effect is accomplished by crosscutting, also called parallel editing, which allows the director to show that events occurring in different spaces are happening simultaneously. There is no logical reason for the audience to assume that the missile is going to destroy the town, but the grammar of the film language and its formalization through eighty years of use encourage this conclusion. Obviously, this type of editing can help to create suspense, as when the camera cuts back and forth between the oncoming train and the car stalled on the tracks.

But crosscutting is not used only to create suspense. This type of editing can also create linkages between characters, themes, or plots. Think about the ending of *The Godfather*. Director Francis Ford Coppola crosscuts from Michael Corleone, attending the baptism of his godchild, to the various brutal murders of his opponents, and back to Michael as he swears to renounce evil. This crosscutting isn't so much about creating suspense as it is to show exactly what kind of man Corleone is and what he is capable of. A film like *Sleepless in Seattle* couldn't exist without crosscutting, because the audience would not be able to see the growing connection between the two characters who have never seen each other. Of course, there are some who argue that this movie shouldn't exist even with the crosscutting.

The Flashback and the Flash-Forward

Like a flashback in literature, this method of connecting shots is designed to give the viewer important information about what has happened in the past. And as with the crosscut, audiences have grown accustomed to the conventions of the flashback and tend to recognize immediately the signals that one is coming up: The characters begin narrating a story ("It all started when . . ."), perhaps they look up or out through a window, maybe some nondiegetic music lightly fades in, and the shot dissolves into another scene, usually with a voice-over of the character still narrating the story. Flashbacks in film tend to happen less regularly than in literature because of the conventions that have to be used, as opposed to a novel that can simply say, "Then he thought back to a time when he was . . . ." It is always interesting in both mediums to examine why a flashback is given at that time: What information does it give to the audience, and who else does not yet have this information? But something that filmmakers can use more regularly than most fiction writers is the flash-forward, which can take the audience ahead of the story's present time. When you look at Chapter 3 of this book, you will see a description of a scene from the film *Elizabeth,* which shows the young queen preparing for a meeting with a hostile group of religious leaders. The scene flashes forward to when the queen arrives at the meeting to face the men, and then it cuts back again to the "present," where she continues her nervous preparation for them. It is clear that this device can add tension and be used as foreshadowing.

The Eye-Line Match

Perhaps one of the most important ways in which shots can be assembled is to connect a series of usually three or more shots to form what's called the eye-line match or point-of-view (POV) shot. The series often begins with a shot of a person looking at something; the camera then cuts to whatever it was that the person was looking at, from that person's perspective, and the series normally ends with a return to the person to show his or her reaction. (See Figure 8 for an illustrative series of three shots taken from the notoriously low-budget film shot in my school's basement.) This type of editing is very important because it can reveal what the character is thinking. Imagine a scene where we see a man standing on a subway platform. First we see him looking around, then the director cuts away to shots of purses dangling from women's arms and wallets sticking out of men's pockets. When the director cuts back to the first man, now smiling, we know, without one word of dialogue, that the man is a thief. In the film *Philadelphia*, a client with AIDS comes into a lawyer's office and, through a series of eye-line matches where we see that the lawyer is watching everything the client touches, we learn that the lawyer is paranoid about the disease and will not take the case. Again, we learn the thoughts of a character without his having said anything. The eye-line match is also a way for a director to create empathy for—or at least a connection to—selected characters, because we ultimately feel what the characters feel when we look through their eyes. Obviously, this is manipulation on the part of the director, but that is his or her job: to make us feel for the characters. This ability to demonstrate the thoughts of characters and to create connections to them through editing is a very important tool for a director, and our recognition of it will become important when we apply film techniques to the study of literature, especially with point of view.

Editing Rhythm and Duration

One final aspect of editing that we ought to consider is not so much *how* the shots are put together, but rather *how long* each shot is permitted to stay on-screen before it gets replaced by another shot through one of the editing techniques described above. The average shot in traditional Hollywood-styled films lasts from about eight to ten seconds. Of course there are plenty of shots that are much shorter or longer, but when a director favors shorter or longer takes (we'll call them "takes" as opposed to shots to avoid confusion with the "long shot," a framing choice described above) the director often does so for a purpose. In a chase sequence, for example, imagine a director crosscutting between the good guys and the bad guys. At first, the takes may last fairly long, say, six seconds or more, but as the good guy catches up and the climax is approaching, the director may choose shorter, quicker takes to create and build suspense, eventually cutting back and forth very quickly so that the takes may last no longer than a second, perhaps even less. MTV became known for the use of rapid-fire editing in the music videos it aired, and many takes on that network last barely a second. This is a method of creating various and repeated images in a very short time period; some people also claimed that it creates headaches in adults and short attention spans in youth, but its influence has become overwhelming

Shot #1

Shot #2

Shot #3

Photos by Ariela Edelman

Figure 8. Usually three shots make up an eye-line match: (1) we see a character looking, (2) we see what he or she is looking at, and (3) we see his or her reaction. This is one of the most important cinematic techniques you can help your students understand.

in film and commercials. Many action sequences use very short takes to capture the rapid pace of the scene: bullets flying, punches being thrown, bystanders running for cover . . .

More significant, perhaps, is the use of the long take. When a shot lasts more than twenty to thirty seconds in contemporary films, it becomes noticeable to the audience and is normally reserved for creating a particular mood or tone. Longer takes can represent a calmer, more peaceful environment, free from distraction and interruption. The final scene in the film *Big Night,* for example, is shot in one take, has almost no dialogue, and lasts over five minutes. The shot becomes almost a sedative for all the craziness that had occurred when the two brothers tried to put on a great party to save their dying restaurant. They failed. But this last scene with its one, long take shows the two brothers coming together, healing old wounds. A cut or any shorter take would have broken the spell of peace and reconciliation. One of the most famous long takes is the opening of Orson Welles's film *Touch of Evil.* In one glorious, three-minute tracking shot, Welles follows a car in which a bomb has been planted as it winds through the crowded streets, twice passes our main characters, and explodes just on the other side of the Mexican border. This complex shot sets up many of the conflicts and themes, as well as the visual and narrative styles, that will be important throughout the rest of the convoluted story. Robert Altman intentionally one-upped Welles in his Hollywood-insider film *The Player,* which begins with an eight-minute tracking shot that does many of the things Welles did, and even includes a character who asks another if he has ever seen the opening of *Touch of Evil.* Editing and rhythm as homage. A final example of an experiment in the long take is Alfred Hitchcock's *Rope,* which contains only eight cuts in the entire eighty-minute film. The cuts themselves are cleverly hidden, so the film appears to consist of one long take. Some critics like to point out that the long take is somehow more natural, closer to how we see the world in reality. I'm not sure that I agree; maybe I'm just hyper, but I'm often jumping back and forth in what I look at, so maybe I see the world as a series of quick jump cuts. Maybe it's the caffeine.

Mise-en-Scène

One of the more difficult film concepts is the idea of mise-en-scène (pronounced "meez-ahn-sen"), and I debated for a long time about including it here. Much has been written about this concept, and entire film philosophies are based on it, but we are going to discuss only what's important to us in the English classroom. The term actually comes from the theater as a way to describe what appears onstage, and when applied to film it refers to some of the elements that a film has in common with the stage: sets, costumes, lighting, and acting. So when we talk about the mise-en-scène of a particular shot or an entire film, we might want to look at what significant props surround the characters, or whether the bad guy wears a black hat, or how the light plays off a character's features. A director includes such important elements in every frame, and for particular purposes, and the concept of mise-en-scène asks us to consider these elements. (See, for example, the shot from *Do the Right Thing* shown in Figure 9 and the shot from *Citizen Kane* shown in Figure 10.) There is much more to this concept than I have covered here, and if you are interested in how mise-en-scène relates to film theory, I recommend that you look at the highly readable *Film Art* (Bordwell and Thompson), which is listed in the resource summary in Appendix C.

Putting It All Together

Simply to introduce this terminology—using the glossary in Appendix C—will not take much longer than a class period, but it is silly to go on too long about film technique without actually showing your students some films. They need practice in identifying the terms and describing how they are used. When you watch any film clip, it is very important that you do not allow the students to simply say, "I saw a long shot" or "That was nondiegetic sound." The film terms themselves mean nothing once they are removed from their *effects.* Instead, students must be encouraged to say, "I saw a low-angle shot that demonstrates _____." Four film clips that are particularly useful for illustrating terminology are discussed below.

Othello (Orson Welles, 1950)

1:15:03–1:18:07

In this scene, Othello, finally driven to action by his rage and jealousy, prepares to murder his faithful wife, Desdemona, while he delivers his famous, "It is the cause, it is the cause" speech from act 5. Welles, who directed and starred as the Moor, shot this version of the play in black and white, and much of this scene plays like something out of a horror film. Luckily for us, it contains examples of most of the film techniques described above. It begins in low-key lighting with a large shot of a growing shadow against a castle wall. The shadow reveals itself to be Othello,

Figure 9. A nice shot to examine for mise-en-scène in Spike Lee's *Do the Right Thing*. Note the lighting of the two young men, their postures, and the surrounding details: wall, radio, graffiti, posters.

Figure 10. This is a perfect example of mise-en-scène in Orson Welles's *Citizen Kane*. The low angle contrasts with the projected image of himself that looms over Kane: Is he powerful? Arrogant?

who is lit only from the side throughout the scene. As he ponders reasons to kill his wife, his face slides in and out of the shadows with the screen going completely dark at times. We then crosscut to a brightly lit Desdemona preparing for bed, and then back to Othello on his way to her bedchamber. At one point, as Othello says, "Yet she must die else she betray more men," the close-up shot of his eyes dissolves into Desdemona's angelic face. Just outside the chamber now, blowing out candles as he goes, Othello walks toward the camera that must have been sunk into the ground because he practically walks over it: an extreme low angle, for sure. You are more than welcome to play the entire scene all the way to Desdemona's murder, but I normally stop it just when Desdemona (front-lit) says, "Who's there? Othello?" and Othello (side-lit so that barely one eye is showing) says, "Ay, Desdemona," and sort of pops up next to her, looking like some creature from the deep. The scene is very creepy and very effective. Again, be sure that your students not only identify the cinematic elements but also explain their effects.

Questions to Consider

1. How are angles used to show power and control?
2. What kind of lighting was used, and for what effect?
3. In the text of *Othello,* there is no mention of Desdemona getting into bed during Othello's speech. Why did Welles crosscut between Othello and Desdemona during this scene? Why did he choose to dissolve between them at times?
4. Identify the diegetic and nondiegetic sounds. What are their effects?

North by Northwest (Alfred Hitchcock, 1958)

1:05:49–1:15:10

This classic cornfield scene has so many cinematic techniques that even if you or your students have already seen it, there are many rich details to examine. To set it up: Cary Grant plays Roger Thornhill, who has been falsely accused of murder and instructed by those who have set him up to come to a deserted field to meet someone named "Kaplan." The sequence begins with an extremely high-angle shot of a bus that stops in the middle of nowhere; a tiny figure gets off as the bus drives away. Next, we see that the figure is Thornhill, and we watch as he looks around at his surroundings. A series of eye-line matches shows that he is absolutely nowhere. There is nothing around him in any direction he looks. As each car approaches, Thornhill tenses up slightly in anticipation, then slumps after it passes him by. There is no nondiegetic sound, and what diegetic sound there is remains very, very quiet, except when the cars pass. We hear the faint sound of a plane buzzing somewhere, but Thornhill pays it no attention—yet. Finally, a car seems to be approaching directly toward us and Thornhill. A man gets out and stands on the opposite side of the road, and, in one of the strangest shots in the film, Hitchcock cuts to a long shot of both men standing in the middle of nowhere facing each other in silence, as if they were suddenly transported to a Western shootout. Is this "Kaplan"? It must be—who else would be out here? As it turns out, though, the man is just waiting for the bus, and, when he leaves, Thornhill is alone again, but that airplane noise is growing louder and louder. The pace of the takes picks up rapidly now as the plane bears down on Thornhill; the plane tries a series of maneuvers in order to kill him, including shooting at him with a machine gun. (See Figure 11 for a classic shot from this sequence.) After escaping into the cornfield for protection, Thornhill is flushed out by crop dust sent down on him, so he has to run back out into the exposed nowhere. A truck is rapidly approaching, and Thornhill waves his arms frantically. Hitchcock crosscuts back and forth between the huge truck bearing down and Thornhill standing in its way, until we see an extreme close-up of the truck's grille and hear the sound of screeching brakes. Thornhill is knocked down just under the truck as it manages to stop. The plane, unable to pull out of its attack, slams into the truck and bursts into flames. We never see the pilot, and now the nondiegetic music kicks in, signifying another close escape by our hero.

Questions to Consider

1. What does Hitchcock do to make this scene suspenseful?
2. How does he show Thornhill's vulnerability?
3. Why does he use only diegetic sound until the very end?

Philadelphia (Jonathon Demme, 1993)

0:22:11–0:29:35

An absolutely wonderful scene in a very good film, this sequence has long been used by Betsy James, a teacher from San Jose, and it illustrates most of the film terms described above. Tom Hanks plays Andrew Beckett, a lawyer who has recently been fired from his high-priced law firm because he has AIDS and who has been trying to find another lawyer to represent him in a case against his former employer. Denzel

Figure 11. The classic cornfield shot from *North by Northwest.* Imagine what would be lost if this were a medium shot or a close-up. Only the long shot can communicate the immediate danger.

Washington plays Joe Miller, a lawyer and a not-so-close acquaintance of Andrew. When Andrew comes into Joe's office, Joe greets him warmly at first, but when Andrew announces that he has AIDS, the camera cuts to a high-angle long shot that shows Joe backing away from him, until he is all the way on the other side of the office, almost in the corner. An uncomfortable silence follows, and the awkward framing and angle are not broken until Andrew asks if he may sit. As they make small talk about Joe's new baby, we see a series of eye-line matches from Joe's point of view that show us a lesion on Andrew's forehead and then we see that Joe is watching everything that Andrew touches—a picture frame, a cigar, a baseball hat—very closely. After some time, during which Joe expresses his skepticism about Andrew's claim that he was sabotaged by the senior partner of his old firm in order to get rid of him, we get a flashback that shows the day that Andrew was fired from his law firm. Andrew is invited into the senior partners' conference room and told by Jason Robards, who plays his boss, that "Everyone here is your friend," yet the chair that has been placed for him is on just about the other side of the room and the room has grown noticeably low-key since he entered. A quickening series of cuts between Andrew and the scowling faces of the partners demonstrates their irrational hostility toward him; the series ends when the camera cuts to the first close-up as Andrew finally asks, "Am I being fired?" When we return to the present, back in Joe's office, the only information that Joe has apparently learned is that Andrew had been concealing his illness, which he refers to as "dreaded, deadly, infectious"; he seemed to ignore or miss the point of the flashback entirely. Perhaps it is because we, the audience, could see what Joe could only hear about. But Joe, of course, turns him down on his offer to take the case, and when he says this, we begin to hear what seem to be diegetic sounds from the street outside slowly growing louder. Just before Andrew leaves, Joe tells him, "Sorry about what happened to you—it's a bitch," but as soon as he's gone, he looks at his hands and gets his secretary to schedule an appointment with his doctor. The street sounds continue to grow louder, and, when we get outside, we see Andrew in a very tight close-up as those diegetic sounds turn into the nondiegetic "The Streets of Philadelphia," in which Bruce Springsteen quietly moans rather than sings. The shot is held in close-up for a very, very long take; people are rushing by Andrew as he stands in front of the office, unable to move, trying not to cry. Everyone has a place to go, but he stays. The camera holds him there. Finally, he leaves, and the camera does not follow. Beautiful.

Questions to Consider

1. Describe the mise-en-scène of Joe's office (pictures of Martin Luther King Jr., big bottle of Rolaids, a window behind him that reads "Toxic") and of the partners' conference room (long tables, similar gray suits, low-key light). What is the effect of these choices?

2. Describe the contrasting uses of the long shot and the close-up in this sequence.

3. Why does this scene include such a variety of editing rhythms? When do you notice the long and quick takes?

4. What information did we get in the flashback that Joe did not? Could this have affected his response to Andrew?

Apocalypse Now (Francis Ford Coppola, 1979)

0:00:00–0:07:27

This film about the Vietnam War is rated R. Please be aware that there is one curse word and a scene of a man drinking alcohol recklessly.

The opening sequence of the film is an absolute must for examining the way that sound can be used to manipulate audience expectations and understandings of what is real or imaginary. It begins with a long shot of a jungle and no sound except for the slow, distorted beating of what seem to be helicopter blades. Slowly, the nondiegetic music ("The End," by the Doors, an interesting choice for the beginning of a film) fades in. Dust and smoke are everywhere. As soon as the lyrics "This is the end, my beautiful friend" are sung, bombs begin to fall, though there still is no other diegetic sound except for those helicopters. The bombs then fall soundlessly. As the camera pans across the destruction, another image—an extreme close-up of an upside-down face—is overlaid on the jungle scene. Technically, it is a dissolve that just hasn't quite finished dissolving, but both images remain on-screen together for several more seconds. Soon the face is replaced by a ceiling fan, which seems to take over the sound of the helicopters that we had been hearing. Now we see that the man is in a room, lying in bed smoking looking up at the ceiling fan, though the jungle images are only now fading away. The camera pans across the man's belongings: cigarettes, liquor bottles, dog tags, a black-and-white picture of a woman, and a gun. The man, we realize, is a soldier on leave, perhaps thinking of the war in the jungle. We cut back to the ceiling fan, which has grown quite loud, though now we realize that the sound may be coming from a helicopter that seems to be landing just outside his window. The sound that was once the helicopters in the jungle became the ceiling fan, and now it becomes a helicopter again. As the man tells us, in a voice-over, that sometimes he wishes he were back in the jungle, we can hear crickets and other jungle sounds slowly creeping in. Are they diegetic? Nondiegetic? Internal diegetic? Difficult to say at this point. The light catches him on the side only, as he appears to be listening to the jungle, though physically he remains in the room; he looks grim and forbidding. The song from the beginning comes back, but now it's crazier, more chaotic, and the man seems to be responding to it. He is moving in time with it, and he smashes a mirror almost simultaneously with a cymbal crash. The scene ends with the man drunk and crying and falling on the floor wearing nothing but a towel.

Questions to Consider

1. If the director's aim was to create a sense of confusion and/or displacement, what elements of the mise-en-scène helped him achieve this?

2. Trace the sounds throughout this scene. Try to classify them as diegetic, internal diegetic, or nondiegetic. Have a reason for your response. When does there seem to be more than one type of sound? What is the effect?

3. How did the lighting and framing choices affect the scene?

Playing Director

In addition to watching films for their terminology, another activity that I like to do with my students is to give them the chance to play director with the terminology and their paper cameras. I break the students into groups of four or five and assign them a particular genre of film (e.g., western, science fiction, kung fu, slapstick comedy) with which they have some familiarity, and I give them five or so film terms that they must demonstrate in a short skit that will be "filmed" by the director and camera operators. Students should quickly write out a script, paying close attention to where their paper cameras will be placed to get the desired effect. Sound and editing should also be considered in their planning. As they act out their scenes, the audience calls out "long shot!" or "nondiegetic!" and afterward we ask the directors why they chose to use those particular shots in those particular ways.

Another activity that I like to do if all the time and resource planets have aligned themselves correctly is to give a group of responsible students a video camera and a hall pass, and ask them to bring back footage illustrating five or so film terms in no more than ten minutes. We can then watch these examples on the same day in class.

There are also those disposable Polaroid cameras that students can use to take still photographs illustrating the film terms. The cameras cost about fifteen dollars and take ten shots each. Again, students will be able to see clearly what the different framing and angle choices achieve. You should know that I hold no stock in the Polaroid company.

However you go about it, the students need to be fully and actively engaged in the meaning behind each of these film terms, or the terms will never mean anything more to them than a list of SAT words. But once students have those terms mastered, they possess a new language, a language that comes complete with analysis and interest already built in. Also, I've noticed that students do not tend to forget these terms or their effects, perhaps because they find daily confirmation of them. Thus it would be worth it to spend a few days in the beginning of the year introducing these terms, so that your students have them available for the rest of the year.

References

Dick, Bernard F. 1998. *Anatomy of Film.* 3rd edition. New York: St. Martin's Press.

Giannetti, Louis. 1999. *Understanding Movies.* 8th edition. Upper Saddle River, NJ: Prentice Hall.

Reflections on Citizen Kane. 1991. Documentary included in *Citizen Kane: Fiftieth Anniversary Limited Collector's Edition.* Turner Home Entertainment.

2 Film and Reading Strategies

As I suggested in the introduction, film and literature are not enemies; in fact, they should be used closely together because they share so many common elements and strategies to gain and keep the audience's attention. We know that for many of our students, film is much more readily accessible than print because of the visual nature and immediacy of the medium, but the very things that films do for us, good and active readers of literature have to do for themselves. With that similarity in mind, this chapter deals primarily with isolating particular skills that we want active readers to possess and demonstrating how they can be introduced and practiced with film *and then* transferred to the written text. This philosophy, I think, reflects most classroom teachers' approach to reader-response theory in that students should try to put themselves into a text before beginning the formal analysis and synthesis. All film does is make this leap easier.

Predicting

When active readers are engaged with a written text, they tend to ask themselves, "What is going to happen next?" We make guesses and, without skipping to the end of the murder mystery—unless you're one of *those*—we revise our predictions as needed. One of the most successful activities for pairing film and literature is to show the opening shots or sequences from a film and ask students to make predictions about what will happen next. I then give students the first page or so of a written text and ask them to make predictions about it. Not only should you have your students predict what they think might happen, but also you must ask them to give several reasons for their guesses. The reasons should be grounded specifically in what they saw or heard. Sure, they might think that *Citizen Kane* or *The Great Gatsby* will be about a wisecracking ski instructor from Venus, but do they have any support for this guess? The point is not that students need to be right about their predictions, but that they make predictions grounded in the film or written text. The sequences described below all work well for predicting because each clip seems to ask more questions than it answers. It is best if you can do at least one film clip and one written text within a given class period, so that students can really see how the process for predicting texts in one medium works equally well for the other.

Citizen Kane (Orson Welles, 1941)

0:00:00–0:02:49

After the sequence opens with a close-up of a "No Trespassing" sign, the camera moves up and over a series of intricately patterned fences and then continues with a long shot of a gloomy-looking dark castle with one lighted window. (See Figure 12 for a very effective shot from this sequence.) The shot dissolves into other long shots of the decrepit grounds, but always with the castle and its one light in the distance. We get a series of long shots connected by very slow dissolves, though we appear to be moving closer and closer to that window. The music is slow and mournful and it seems to be building to a climax just as the light goes out. And as it does, we have moved, subtly, inside that room; we have now officially trespassed. Next, we see a close-up of a hand holding a snow globe that depicts a scene of a small cabin. The snow seems to fill not just the globe but the whole frame as well. The only spoken word in the whole sequence is when a man—shot in an extreme close-up of just his mouth—whispers "Rosebud" and dies. The glass ball drops from his hand and shatters, without a diegetic crashing sound, on the floor. A nurse calmly enters the room and covers him with a sheet. We see one more shot of his body lengthwise and deep in shadows before the scene and the music fade out.

Questions to Consider

1. What is Rosebud? (No fast forwarding if you don't know.) How do you know it's important?

2. Who is this man, and why is his death important to this film? What will it be about?

3. What visual clues did Welles give us to create the mood or theme of this film?

4. What is the significance of beginning with the "No Trespassing" sign?

Rear Window (Alfred Hitchcock, 1954)

0:00:00–0:04:34

As the titles run (and, by the way, your kids will need to be reminded that the opening credits are part of the film; they're so used to getting popcorn or talking during them), we see the large windows of an apartment

Fig. 12. The lighting and music that accompany the opening shots of *Citizen Kane* create the somber mood, and the presence of the gates and the lighted window of the looming castle create a sense of spying and trespassing.

building and the blinds are slowly being raised by some unseen hand. There is a lively (nondiegetic?) jazz soundtrack playing. After the credits, the camera slowly tracks forward, toward and nearly out of one of those windows, which, we see now, looks out onto a middle-class apartment courtyard. (See Figure 13 for a publicity still from the film.) The camera pans across the apartment windows directly across from where we started and shows the neighbors getting ready in the morning to the tune of that jazz we heard from the credits. Slowly we come back inside the first apartment again to see a close-up of a man sleeping and sweating. Cutting to a thermometer, we see it's over 90 degrees. Closer than the first time it did so, the camera again pans across the courtyard and now we can make out some detail. First we see a man shaving, and that song we had been hearing turns out to have been coming from his radio (so it was actually diegetic), which now plays a commercial. He switches stations and the new tune fills the courtyard. We see a couple sleeping on the fire escape and a young woman who dresses in front of her open window and makes coffee while stretching her legs. Returning another time to the first apartment, we now see that the man is in a wheelchair with a cast on his leg that reads, "Here lie the broken bones of L. B. Jefferies." In a series of close-ups, the camera dollies and pans across the man's possessions: a broken camera, action photographs on the wall, a framed picture of a woman seen in negative, and a stack of fashion magazines. Is it the same woman? It looks a little like the woman across the courtyard. No answers yet because the scene ends at that point with a slow fade to black.

Questions to Consider

1. Why so many long shots? Why the use of only diegetic sound?
2. Who will be the main character, and how do you know this?
3. Who will the minor characters be, and what role do you think they will play?
4. What role will the setting play in this film?

Ghost (Jerry Zucker, 1990)

0:00:00–0:03:45

This is kind of an interesting film to show even if students have already seen it, because it really asks them to pay attention to the visual and sound elements in order to make good predictions. This clip was recommended to me by Ann Foster, a teacher in Brevard County, Florida. When you use this sequence be sure to begin right at the very beginning

Fig_re 13. The setting for the action in _Rear Window_: the normal and the everyday go bad.

because the word "GHOST" appears suddenly, flashes twice (punctuated by the nondiegetic music), and quickly disappears. The camera then moves through what appears to be an attic filled with dusty, forgotten items. The lighting is classic low-key with shafts of light coming through the walls, ceiling, and floor. It is rather disorienting, and the objects that the camera shows us are all somewhat indistinct: bundles of miscellaneous items, as well as wires and pipes, but nothing is clear. The camera then moves to an area of total darkness, which is suddenly punctured by a hole being smashed in what we now realize is the floor of the attic room we have been looking at. Three figures, all in white, look into the space. Next, we see those same figures swinging sledgehammers at a wall, which goes down inside that room where we had been. When they move into the space, one of the men finds a jar with an "Indian-head" penny inside, which he proclaims as "a good omen." A woman responds, "You're the good omen," and gives him a big hug. "It's so great," the woman says just at the end of the scene. Using the title, the atmosphere, and what preconceptions they have, your students should be able to make some interesting, though perhaps incorrect, predictions.

Questions to Consider

1. Listen again, and closely, to the music at the very beginning. Is it standard ghost-story music, or are there other elements? Describe its effect.

2. What specific elements seem to be foreshadowing? What do you think they foreshadow?

3. Why do you think the director started with us inside the attic? What is the effect of that choice?

Shifting to Print Texts

Now you should take the opening paragraph or two of any novel or story (e.g., "Call me Ishmael" or "It was the best of times . . .") and have students take exactly the same approach. It is best if you use a novel that they are actually going to be reading for class, so that they can reassess their predictions from time to time. (The sample chart in Figure 14 is from a class prediction based on the first chapter of *Their Eyes Were Watching God*. As you can see, students' guesses may be right or wrong, but they do have textual support for their predictions.) Also note one more thing: there is almost nothing in common that I can think of between *Kane* and *Their Eyes*, but that is the point. We are isolating skills that our students can apply to any text they encounter.

Film/Novel	Predictions about Character, Theme, Setting	Reasons for Predictions
Citizen Kane, directed by Orson Welles	This is going to be a murder mystery. We are going to find out who poisoned the old man. The old man is very rich and lonely. I bet that he has a lot of children who don't come to visit him too much.	I think it's going to be a mystery because of the dark lighting and the creepy music. I think that he's lonely because he's in a big old house and when he died, the nurse didn't cry or anything.
Their Eyes Were Watching God by Zora Neale Hurston	I think that this is going to be a girl's book. I think the story is going to be about that woman who is coming into the town and what will happen to her when the town hears about what she did.	It talks about love and dreams and horizons and things like a girl would talk about. She's going to be the main character because we hear a lot of descriptions about her good body and how the town is jealous of her.

Figure 14. Prediction chart.

Responding to the Text

We know that, in addition to making predictions about a text, active readers make a text their own. But how do they do this, and how can we assist those students who may not be inclined to do so? One of the best methods I have found is to have students keep a type of viewing/reading log (see Figure 15 for an example) as they read short passages and watch film clips. As with the prediction activity, this one is best used when mixed in with short prose passages or even poems. In fact, this exercise is almost best viewed as a sort of drill-and-practice because we want these kinds of responses to become almost second nature to students. I try to sandwich two reading passages between two short film clips, alternating between the reading and the viewing. I start with a high-interest film clip, move to a high-interest reading clip, then look at a more challenging viewing text, and follow with a difficult reading selection. (If you look at the sample chart shown in Figure 15, you'll see that when I ask students to respond, I want them to think about their

Film/Story/Poem	I liked . . .	It reminded me of . . .	I felt confused when . . .
A Christmas Story, directed by Bob (Benjamin) Clark	when the kid said the bad word, but we didn't really hear it. I liked it when the mother called his friend's mom.	a time when I got grounded for pushing my little brother and I got sent to my room. I hated my dad then.	I didn't get why the kid was wearing glasses and carrying a cane, but I figured it out.
"Those Winter Sundays" by Robert Hayden	the phrases: "no one ever thanked him" and the "angers of the house."	My father used to wake up early during the summer and mow the lawn at like 7:00 a.m. The neighbors hated us.	What does "love's austere and lonely offices" mean? Is the father a nice guy or an angry guy?
Henry V, directed by Kenneth Branagh	I didn't like much except for when she tried to speak English words and got them wrong.	It reminded me of why I dropped Spanish last year; I hate trying to speak other languages.	Just about everything. It took me about five minutes just to realize what was going on and by that time the clip was over. Are we going to see it again?
"Chicago" by Carl Sandburg	many of the really visual lines: "Flinging magnetic curses" and "fierce as a dog."	the inner city. I thought about the homeless people I see downtown.	I couldn't figure out who the guy talking is. He loves Chicago, but why does he say all the bad things about it?

Figure 15. Sample viewing/reading log.

connection—or their lack of connection, which is just as important to identify—to the selected text.) The questions are simple: What did you like or not like about it? What does this text remind you of? When did you feel confused or uninterested? Just as with the prediction exercises, this activity should focus mainly on the skills that it takes to be an involved viewer/reader. The questions that follow each clip are not necessarily analytical in nature, but rather they are intended to encourage personal response to the text.

High-Interest Film #1: *A Christmas Story*
(Bob [Benjamin] Clark, 1983)

0:39:02–0:45:00

A wonderful clip from my favorite Christmas movie (sorry, Jimmy Stewart), this sequence begins as Ralphie, an eight-year-old boy, and his family are driving back from buying a Christmas tree when the car gets a flat tire. While helping his father change the tire, Ralphie accidentally drops the lug nuts and, worse, yells "Fudge!" in front of his father. The voice-over narration, however, points out that he didn't actually say "fudge," but a curse word that begins with the same letter. (Don't worry—he doesn't actually say it.) At home his mother puts a bar of soap in his mouth until he tells her who taught him the bad word. Since he cannot, of course, tell her that he heard it from his own father, he blames a friend of his. Angry at his punishment, Ralphie imagines a scene later in life when he returns home as a blind man, blinded by the very soap his parents forced him to swallow. His fantasy ends with his parents begging his forgiveness, and the scene ends with Ralphie back in bed feeling better at the thought.

Questions to Consider

1. What was the funniest moment of the scene? What made it funny?
2. When have you been in a situation similar to Ralphie's, whether getting in trouble, receiving punishment, or fantasizing about retribution through guilt?
3. How did the voice-over narration help you follow the story?
4. What was the most interesting framing choice in the sequence? Why?

High-Interest Film #2: *Groundhog Day* **(Harold Ramis, 1993)**

0:45:56–0:56:20

In this sequence, a television weatherman, Phil, played by Bill Murray, has become trapped in some sort of twilight zone where he is forced to repeat the same day (February 2) over and over, though no one else is aware that it has been Groundhog Day again and again. Perhaps out of genuine interest or perhaps because he simply is bored, Phil tries to begin a romance with his producer, Rita, played by Andie McDowell. He is not at all successful at first, but, remember, he has day after day to improve his pickup lines. And she has no recollection of the previous night's date. Each little sequence within this scene moves Phil closer and closer to having Rita fall in love with him, but he always messes up something. At one point, while they are dancing, the nondiegetic song "You Don't Know Me" by Ray Charles seems to signal that Phil's attempts are shallow and ultimately unsuccessful. Toward the end of the scene, Rita turns him down in his hotel room, and the remainder of the scene recounts several repeated days of Phil's attempting just to get their date back to the hotel room. His attempts to plan and reinvent the spontaneity of the first night are quite pitiful, and, after a series of rapidly edited face slaps that happen earlier and earlier in the date, Phil finally gives up.

Questions to Consider

1. When did you laugh the most? When did you feel sorry for either character?

2. If you could live one day over and over, what would you do with your time? Did Phil accomplish anything worthwhile during his repeated days in this sequence?

3. Would you get bored with life if you had to live it like this? When did Phil appear to be bored?

4. How did the editing contribute to the humor in this scene?

Challenging Film #1: *Henry V* (Kenneth Branagh, 1989)

0:51:15–0:55:09

First of all, this scene is almost entirely in French. Emma Thompson plays Katherine, the daughter of the French king, who wants to learn English and asks Alice, her maid, to teach her the English words for various body parts. There are no subtitles whatsoever, so unless you speak French, you have to figure out what you can from the context, the actions, and the heavily accented English words they do say. As Katherine and Alice practice the words, Katherine giggles and dances around like a schoolgirl. The scene ends as Katherine opens the door to her chamber, laughing at her new vocabulary, as her father, the dour king, walks by, obviously heavy with thoughts of the coming war with England.

Questions to Consider

1. Have you ever seen a foreign film with subtitles? Did you expect this one to have subtitles? How did you feel when you realized that there were not going to be any?

2. What were the words that Katherine learned? Were these similar to or different from the first words that you learned in a foreign language?

3. When did you feel the most confused during this scene? When did you really feel like you understood what they were talking about? Do you think that you would understand even more if you were to see the clip again?

Challenging Film #2: *The Conversation* (Francis Ford Coppola, 1974)

0:33:05–0:39:36

This is a difficult sequence for a number of reasons. It can be difficult to follow the plot itself, which occurs in a present time and a series of flashbacks, and it also takes quite a bit of time to understand what the characters in the flashbacks are saying—which actually is the point of the entire scene. Harry, played by Gene Hackman, is a surveillance expert who has been hired, apparently by a jealous husband, to audiotape a conversation between a man and woman as they discuss their affair. Before this scene begins, Harry has already turned in a transcript of the tape to his employer, but something still nags at him, and in this sequence he tries to work on the audio quality in order to hear their entire conversation more clearly. So, as he works on the tape, we *see* visual flashbacks of the man and the woman talking even though Harry himself can only *hear* them talk. Gradually, the sound becomes clearer and Harry becomes increasingly interested in getting every word. All the while, we have been seeing different angles and framings of the conversation as Harry works on the dialogue. Finally, the key phrase in the entire conversation has been made out: the man says to the woman, "He'd kill us if he got the chance." Everything that was said earlier now takes on a different meaning. It may be a case not only of adultery but also of murder. If you let the scene play just another second or two, you will see that Harry immediately goes to a church for confession and guidance.

Questions to Consider

1. When were you most confused or bored with this scene? When were you most interested? Why?

2. How would this scene have been different if we did not see the conversation, but, like Harry, only heard it?

3. When have you overheard a conversation and been interested in what the participants were saying?

4. What do you think Harry will do about what he heard?

This activity values a type of viewer (or reader) reaction that is often looked down on: the simple response. Too often I hear myself saying to my students, "Don't tell me your feelings about it; give me an analysis of it!" I forget sometimes that in order to analyze a text, students must first interact with it at the most basic level, and, when I ignore that step, the result is that the students are cut off from the text, unable to do much with it at all. These exercises, then, remind us that when a student says, "I didn't like it," they are beginning the process of making meaning out of that text—an important first step.

Questioning the Text

Once students have begun responding to the text, we can now move them toward a greater interaction with it. An effective way to get started is to have students write questions about the text you are studying. The act of *asking* questions, rather than simply *answering* questions all the time, is essential to achieving a real connection with a text. Think about a typical student's day, in which all he or she does is answer questions posed by adults in authority. But when students begin to question the text, they gain ownership of it, and become, in fact, an authority. In order to help make their questions as focused and relevant as possible, I recommend introducing students to the idea of the levels of questions. This approach was presented to me by two California English teachers, Jo Ellen Victoreen and Betsy James, who synthesized the ideas of various Great Books programs and the College Board's Building Success strategies. The main idea is that there are three levels of questions that can be asked about any text, and all three types of questions are essential to being able to construct meaning from the text. Students should be taught about these levels and encouraged to write questions at each of them.

Level One: Questions of Fact

These questions can be answered with a word, phrase, or detail from the text. Imagine reading the story of Cinderella. A level one question might be, "What time must Cinderella be home?" or "What was turned into her carriage?" Sometimes these are basic recall questions to check on comprehension, but they are not always simple questions; in fact, at times they are essential to gathering support for an argument.

Level Two: Questions of Interpretation

These questions can be answered only by interpreting the facts given in or suggested by the text. Again from Cinderella: "What motivated Cinderella to want to go the ball?" or "How would you characterize her stepsisters?" These are the kinds of questions that we often ask in our classrooms, addressing such concerns as character, setting, and tone. They can also involve authorial/directorial intent in using a particular phrase, angle, lighting choice, or other technique or element: "Why did the director use [particular device or technique]?"

Level Three: Questions Beyond the Text

These are questions that relate some aspect of the text to the real world. Answers to these questions are to be found not by looking within this single text but by examining society and the world at large. With Cinderella, a level three question might be, "Why are women often portrayed as waiting for Prince Charming to save them?" or "Is there such a thing as 'happily ever after'?"

Notice that each of these three levels is essential to interacting with a text, and none of them is any more significant than the others, even though the numbering implies a hierarchy of sorts. Also remember that since this exercise asks the students themselves to come up with the questions, they should take the lead in the discussions that follow. Or, you may not even want to have their questions answered; sometimes the questions alone are enough. Just as with the two previous activities, the idea is to use the film clips to practice writing good questions at each level and then move on to the written text. Below are outlines for several film clips, along with sample questions I have created for each level. The chart shown in Figure 16 includes sample questions that I received from students when we did this activity at the beginning of our study of *Romeo and Juliet*, using *Titanic* as a lead-in.

Titanic (James Cameron, 1987)

0:55:39–1:03:00

This sequence in the first third of the doomed-boat film deals with third-class passenger Jack Dawson, played by Leonardo DiCaprio, when he is invited by first-class passenger Rose, played by Kate Winslet, to dinner in the main dining room. The scene begins as Jack is being dressed in appropriate attire by the kindly Molly Brown. When he enters the first-class section, Jack is initially awed and a little intimidated by the surroundings of the main foyer and the dining room, as well as by the

Titles	Questions
Titanic	Level One: Where does Jack get his nice suit of clothes? Why is he eating dinner with the rich people?
	Level Two: Why does Rose like Jack? How is he different from her boyfriend?
	Level Three: Why do rich people look down on poor people? Does money make you happier?
Romeo and Juliet (Act 1)	Level One: Who is Romeo in love with at first? Who are the two feuding families?
	Level Two: What makes Romeo fall in love so quickly? What will be the most difficult thing for Romeo to overcome in order to get Juliet?
	Level Three: Is love supposed to be difficult? Why do people meddle in other people's lives?

Figure 16. Levels of questioning.

gestures expected of a gentleman, which, as it is pointed out to him by Rose's fiancé, he is only pretending to be. Soon enough, however, Jack begins to gain confidence and, in fact, dominates the conversation at the dinner table with his rough eloquence. Notice the cutaways to Rose and Molly, showing their admiration. The scene ends as the guests at the table all raise their glasses to echo a statement Jack has made about "Making it count!"

Level One

1. How does Jack say that he got his ticket for the *Titanic*?
2. What items at the dinner table does Jack have the most difficulty with?

Level Two

1. Why does the mother appear to be threatened by Jack? Why does Cal appear *not* to be threatened by him?
2. What does Jack seem to value most?

3. What does the director do to make us sympathize with Jack?

Level Three

1. Do you think that there is as much difference between the social classes today as there was in the time of the film?
2. What does it mean to "make it count"? Do you or people you
know seem to live their lives like Jack does?

Smoke Signals (Chris Eyre, 1998)

0:33:50–0:38:10

I absolutely love this short scene from this small independent film,
which was, by the way, one of the first major releases to have a predomi-
nantly American Indian cast and crew. Victor and Thomas are teenagers taking their first major trip away from their reservation in Coeur
d'Alene, on their way to collect some items left by Victor's father, who
recently died and who had disappeared from the family years ago. On
the bus, Victor tries to teach Thomas, a geeky boy with braids who smiles
all the time, what it means to be "a real Indian." He tells him to be stoic
and to imagine that he has just come back from killing a buffalo. In addition, his hair needs to be long and free, to show his power. This is the
only way, Victor says, that the Whites will leave them alone. A few
moments later we see the bus driver and Victor waiting alongside the
bus as Thomas comes out of the restroom in slow motion, hair flowing
wild and a look of stone on his face. It lasts only so long, as he breaks
out into one of his smiles again. The smile doesn't last long either, however, because when they get back on the bus, two White men have taken
their seats and refuse to move for them. Victor tries to be tough and use
the stoic face, but the men only respond with racial insults. Thomas and
Victor take new seats, and, though Thomas tries to tease him gently
about the "Indian power," both boys are clearly hurt. They do, however, get some revenge by singing about John Wayne's teeth. (If you like
this clip, be sure to consider teaching the complete film; see Chapter 4.)

Level One

1. What does "stoic" mean? What is a stoic face like?
2. When Thomas tells Victor that their tribe never hunted buffalo, what does he say they did hunt?

Level Two

1. How does Victor feel about his American Indian heritage? How
is this different from how Thomas feels?

2. What is the effect of the long, slow-motion shot of Thomas coming out of the rest room? Describe how the nondiegetic music helped create this effect.

3. Why do Thomas and Victor not do more to get the men out of their seats?

Level Three

1. What does the popular representation of American Indians tend to be like in the media today, and what has it been like throughout history?

2. What do you think is the most common misunderstanding between Whites and American Indians?

3. What causes racism between various ethnic and racial groups?

The Color Purple (Steven Spielberg, 1985)

0:19:41–0:22:48

Very early on in this adaptation of Alice Walker's novel, Celie is young but already married to a brutal man called Mister. Her sister Nettie has come to live with them, and the sisters become inseparable (as seen in the shot shown in Figure 17), though they know that Nettie will have to leave soon because Celie's husband, played by Danny Glover, is looking at her in a way unbecoming of a brother-in-law. This clip begins when Nettie and Celie are talking about staying in touch somehow. When Celie says that they can write to each other, Nettie decides to teach her older sister to read by placing the names of things all around the house. Together they spell things like jar and kettle, but when Celie gets to "sky," she spells "M-i-s-t-e-r" instead because her husband is suddenly there towering over them, glaring down at her. The scene continues as they run around like school children playing games and hugging each other, but it ends when Mister, not quite reading the paper he's holding, eyes Nettie even more closely.

Level One

1. Why does Nettie teach Celie to read?
2. What do they carve into the tree alongside the house?

Level Two

1. Why do you think Mister does not want Celie to learn to read?
2. What do you think the sunflowers the girls play with represent?

Figure 17. From *The Color Purple*: the young Celie and Nettie in happy times, as represented by the high-key light and the lush fields.

3. What does the director do to make us feel the closeness of the sisters in this scene? Why is it important for us to feel that?

4. How does the director show us Mister's growing interest in Nettie?

Level Three

1. At its most basic level, as in this scene, why is education so important?

2. Are there differences between the ways that men and women are educated?

3. What roles do siblings play in our lives?

The most important part of this activity is the fact that it is up to the students to generate questions on the three levels for each of the film clips. When they write the questions in this manner, they have to be engaged with the clip on a variety of levels, and, in fact, they become the experts on the text. After you have practiced this approach a few times with these or other film clips, you will see how well students are able to question a written text. When I am in the middle of a novel with my classes, I often have them generate questions for quizzes and use their level three questions for journal topics. I also put students in charge of a chapter to present and discuss their questions with the rest of the class. It has almost always been successful, I promise.

Storyboarding

One of the greatest successes I have had in using film study as a reading strategy is to ask students to "storyboard" a portion of the story or novel we are reading. These storyboards are graphic representations of exactly what would appear in each shot in a film adaptation of the text we're reading. It's sort of like a comic strip, though there are no dialogue balloons or "?#@@&*&?!!!" type of symbols anywhere on the picture since it is supposed to look exactly like the finished film image on the movie screen would look. The storyboard is essential in determining framing, angles, and many other choices, and just about all directors will storyboard most of their shots ahead of time in order to be sure that their ideas turn out the way they had intended. (Many digital video disks [DVDs] available for rental or purchase now include the storyboards used while filming the movie.) It is legend that Hitchcock rarely looked through the lens of the camera for any of his films because he had storyboarded every shot so extensively that there simply was no need: he could see it all in pictures in front of him. Even though real storyboards are drawn by professional artists, our storyboards will not require any artistic talent whatsoever. The idea is to ask the students to imagine how a story might be filmed and to represent their ideas visually, and stick figures work just as well as more polished pieces. There are two similar types of storyboard assignments that I like to do with my students. The first is a close reading of particular lines that I have in mind from a text we are reading, and the students complete a chart like the one shown in Figure 18, which is based on a text selection I have had good success with—the opening of "The Fall of the House of Usher," which reads as follows:

> During the whole of a dull, dark, and soundless day in the autumn of the year, when the clouds hung oppressively low in the heavens, I had been passing alone, on horseback, through a singularly dreary tract of country; and at length found myself, as the shades of the evening drew on, within view of the melancholy House of Usher. I know not how it was—but, with the first glimpse of the building, a sense of insufferable gloom pervaded my spirit. I say insufferable; for the feeling was unrelieved by any of that half-pleasurable, because poetic, sentiment, with which the mind usually receives even the sternest natural images of the desolate or terrible. I looked upon the scene before me—upon the mere house, and the simple landscape features of the domain—upon the bleak walls—upon the vacant eye-like windows—upon a few rank sedges—and upon a few white trunks of decayed trees—with an utter depression of soul which I can compare to no earthly sensation more properly than to the afterdream of the reveler upon opium—the bitter lapse into common life—the hideous dropping off of the veil. There was an iciness, a sinking, a sickening of the heart—an unredeemed dreariness of thought which no goading of the imagination could torture into aught of the sublime. What was it—I paused to think—what was it that so unnerved me in the contemplation of the House of Usher? It was a mystery all insoluble; nor could I grapple with the shadowy fancies that crowded upon me as I pondered. I was forced to fall back upon the unsatisfactory conclusion, that while, beyond a doubt, there *are* combinations of very simple natural objects which have the power of thus affecting us, still the reason, and the analysis of this power lies among considerations beyond our depth. It was possible, I reflected, that a mere different arrangement of the particulars of the scene, of the details of the picture, would be sufficient to modify, or perhaps to annihilate its capacity for sorrowful impression; and, acting upon this idea, I reined my horse to the precipitous brink of a black and lurid tarn that lay in unruffled luster by the dwelling, and gazed down—but with a shudder even more thrilling than before—upon the remodeled and inverted images of the gray sedge, and the ghastly tree-stems, and the vacant and eye-like windows.

FILM & READING STRATEGIES:
STORYBOARDING ACTIVITY # 1

	What did you want to demonstrate?	What lines helped you see this?

SHOT #1

I wanted to show the gloominess of the setting, which is like a cemetery or something.

"autumn of the year"
"clouds hung oppressively low"
"dreary tract of country"

SHOT #2

I wanted to show that the narrator has come upon a very sad and broken-down old house.

"bleak walls"
"vacant eye-like windows"
"rank sedges"

SHOT #3

The narrator is immediately repulsed by the house and I wanted to show his horrified reaction to it.

"a sense of insufferable gloom invaded my spirit."

What music or sound effects would you imagine in this scene? Why?

If this really were a movie, I would want a slow-moving classical song with lots of violins playing. We would hear only the sounds of the horse moving along the path. But when he first sees the house, there is no sound at all.

Figure 18. Chart for first storyboarding activity.

Nevertheless, in this mansion of gloom I now proposed to myself a sojourn of some weeks. Its proprietor, Roderick Usher, had been one of my boon companions in boyhood; but many years had elapsed since our last meeting. A letter, however, had lately reached me in a distant part of the country—a letter from him—which, in its wildly importunate nature, had admitted of no other than a personal reply. The MS. gave evidence of nervous agitation. The writer spoke of acute bodily illness—of a pitiable mental idiosyncrasy which oppressed him—and of an earnest desire to see me, as his best, and indeed his only personal friend, with a view of attempting, by the cheerfulness of my society, some alleviation of his malady. It was the manner in which all this, and much more, was said—it was the apparent *heart* that went with his request—which allowed me no room for hesitation; and I accordingly obeyed what I still considered a very singular summons, forthwith.

Based on selected lines from this excerpt (or from whatever other text we may be using), students draw what they imagine would be on-screen during this part of the story, and they must be able to explain what in the story itself led them to make this particular choice. In other words, if they used a close-up or a low-angle shot of the house, what language that Poe used made them imagine the house that way? Not only do they need to visualize the language of the story, but they also must begin interpreting the reasons why Poe might have used a particular word or phrase. This activity, I have found, is best done while you are at the very beginning of your study of the text because it becomes such an engaging entrance into the story.

The second storyboarding activity is a little more creative and wide-ranging. After we have read a short story or a novel, I select a chapter or a portion of a chapter and assign one student, or a group of students working together, the task of completing a chart such as Storyboard Activity #2 (see Figure 19). You can see the differences between these two activities. The first depends on a close reading of the text itself, whereas the second allows for greater individual interpretation. This second activity also requires students to have a full knowledge of cinematic technique, since it asks them about camera movement, editing, lighting, and so on. Obviously it still requires a close reading of the text, but it also gives the students much more flexibility in deciding which lines from the story are the most relevant or have the best visual connection. The two shots sampled here are taken, again, from "The Fall of the House of Usher," though I normally ask for anywhere between five and ten shots to be storyboarded. When you break the text into sections and assign them to groups to present, the whole story gets retold visually. Whichever activity you use, it is important that students, acting as directors, are aware of the effects their choices have and know that those choices should have at least some basis in the original text.

It is very important to reemphasize that artistic skill is not required to create a good storyboard. What your students are trying to demon-

FILM & READING STRATEGIES:
STORYBOARDING ACTIVITY # 2

Title: "House of Usher"   **Pages:** 1–2

Summary of Scene:
This starts just as the narrator reins his horse and begins
to walk down to the house.

SHOT # 1

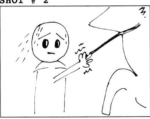

Intended Effect of Shot:
To show that the house appears
forgotten and overgrown.
Diegetic Sound:
wind blowing, horse stomping, an owl
screeching
Non-diegetic Sound:
scary, horror-movie, very
dramatic and fast paced.

Shot Type: long shot

Angle: low angle

Movement: pan to house

Lighting:
very low key, especially dark around
the house.

Edit: dissolve to #2

SHOT # 2

Intended Effect of Shot:
To show that the narrator is deeply
affected just by the sight of the
house.
Diegetic Sound:
The narrator shivers, the horse
stomps even louder, and the wind is
now howling.
Non-diegetic Sound:
Same as shot #1, but now it is
building to a crescendo that will
continue until he enters the house.

Shot Type: medium

Angle: high angle

Movement: none

Lighting:
low key with side lighting on the
narrator to emphasize his fear.

Edit: cut to #3

Figure 19. Chart for second storyboarding activity.

strate are their interpretations, represented in visual images, of a written text. It is amazing to see how each student will visualize and adapt the same story differently. As a culminating activity, you may want to show students a filmed version of the story they have read so that they can see the similarities and differences between their interpretations and those of professional filmmakers. Many suitable videos of stories are probably available in your school's library; for example, I know that McDougal Littell has a series, and the American Short Story collection from PBS is widely available. Whenever I have shown a filmed version of a text that we have storyboarded, invariably some students will loudly protest that the professional filmmakers got it all wrong and that theirs were better. That's definitely taking some ownership of a text!

Soundtrack

Another great way to engage students with a text is to ask them to imagine being the producer of a film being made of whatever story you are reading in class. One of the tasks of the producer is to find songs and musical accompaniment that will go along with the story.

If you were reading "The Cask of Amontillado," for example, you might make a tape of three or four short songs, or portions of songs, that you think might be appropriate. The songs I have used for this particular story are "Welcome to the Jungle" by Guns N' Roses, "The Adversary" by Crime and the City Solution, and any classical piece that sounds a little mournful (see Figure 20 for sample student responses about how the songs might be used). As you play each song, ask your students the following questions:

1. Where would this song fit best in a movie of this story? What *action* would be happening on screen while this song was playing? Why at this place?

2. What would the scene look like while this song was playing? Shot type? Angle? Lighting? Why these?

3. If you could select only one of these songs, which one would you choose? Why?

This type of exercise, again, asks your students to visualize the written text, but it also requires that they know enough about the characters, setting, and plot of the story to be able to justify their choices. After you have gone through the music selections you brought to class, ask students what songs they know of that might fit the story. Believe me, they will be able to think of great ones; maybe, too, you can convince them to bring in music to share, and maybe even to copy it for you so you can use it next year. This activity does take a little time, in order to find appropriate songs for a written text, but it pays off wonderfully. (In fact, I've expanded this activity while writing this book. Recently I asked students to put together an entire soundtrack—four or five songs—for a novel we were reading, along with a brief explana-

Song Title	Where would it go in the story? Why?	What specific images do you imagine?
"The Adversary" by Crime and the City Solution	This would happen just when Montressor chains him up because Fortunado now knows he is the enemy and the song tells him that.	A close-up of the bricks being put in place and the smile of Montressor.
"Love's Illusion" by Anonymous 4	I bet this would go at the beginning when he is telling his plans because it seems like it would be from that time period. It's old and classical, but also kind of haunting.	Maybe we would see establishing shots of the whole city as the camera pans across the buildings. It stops on Montressor's window and we go inside.
"Welcome to the Jungle" by Guns N' Roses	I don't know, it sounds kind of out of place, but it's very loud and the guy singing it seems crazy so it should probably go just when Montressor and Fortunado first go into the catacombs since he says "Welcome."	It should be very dark, and the camera should be sort of jumping all over the place. Fortunado's cap, Montressor's evil smile, etc.

- Now, as the film's producer, you just found out that your budget allows for only *one* of the above songs. Which one would you choose, and why?

- What other songs that you know of would fit in well with this story? Where would they fit?

Figure 20. Soundtrack possibilities for "The Cask of Amontillado."

tion of why they chose the songs they did. We shared the soundtracks in class and debated which were more effective.)

The ideas behind each of these activities derive, really, from garden-variety reading strategies; there's no rocket science or critical theory here. Anytime we can get our students fully involved in a text, we know we have done our job. The particular skills—predicting, responding, questioning, and visualizing—are ones that students at any level need either to develop or to practice. I have found that students are more willing to practice with film at first, and then they may follow you by swallowing that bitter pill of reading the written text as well. We just won't tell them that reading the text was the whole point anyway.

Reference

Poe, Edgar Allan. 1983. "The Fall of the House of Usher." *The Unabridged Edgar Allan Poe*. Philadelphia: Running Press.

3 Film and Literary Analysis

Ideally, in our perfect reader-response world, the students have immersed themselves successfully in the text through the activities in Chapter 2, so the next step should be to help them move on to analysis and synthesis. Toward that end, this chapter discusses ways to help students practice using analytical skills in considering films and then—we hope—apply those skills to their work with literature. There are many aspects of literature that we want our students to be able to analyze, but the most common ones, and those which have ready connections to film, are characterization, setting, point of view (POV), symbol, and irony. This chapter's structure resembles that of Chapter 2, offering a discussion of possible films to examine, along with sample student charts of literary and cinematic analysis.

Characterization

When we talk about analyzing literature for characterization, we are trying to find out what defines, motivates, or is unique about a particular character. Aspects that we focus on as significant in literature include actions, thoughts, emotions, and speech, as well as other details such as age and physical appearance. We also want students to focus on how the writer helps to create or develop this character through various literary techniques. What we want students to do in terms of analyzing literary characterization, then, has some obvious parallels to considerations of characterization in film.

Elizabeth (Shekhar Kapur, 1998, rated R)

0:52:08–0:57:23

Prior to this scene, Elizabeth, played by Cate Blanchett, is young and not at all stable in her reign. She has many powerful enemies, chief among them the Catholic priests. In this scene, we see her as she first prepares for and then confronts the English clergymen about a proposal that would reinstate her as the head of the Church of England, which they oppose because of the separation it would cause between themselves and the Pope in Rome. At first, Elizabeth is shown in a high-key medium shot, wearing a plain white dressing gown as she practices delivering her speech, changing words and phrases along the way. It is not going well, and she becomes frustrated and scared. The takes are quick and the cuts seem jarring. The director then does a type of crosscut flash-forward, in which we see the gathered clergy, moving aside as she enters, shot in low-key lighting from a low angle—that is, from Elizabeth's perspective—thus emphasizing their strength and her fear. We then cut back and forth several times between her practicing and her arrival the next day. When she ascends her throne in front of the clergy, she is now wearing royal red ("her power suit," as one of my students called it), but she is framed almost entirely with long shots from above and behind several people's heads. The effect of this framing is that we cannot make her out too clearly in the crowd; she gets lost amid the men. Initially, the meeting does not go well, but as she gains more control through her verbal wit, the camera begins to frame her with more medium shots. By the end, when she talks about what is right for "my people," the camera finally shoots her from a low angle, framed in a close-up, straight on without anything blocking her, and the nondiegetic music begins and swells as it announces her victory over the clergy. Power has changed; she is in control.

Questions to Consider

1. What was the purpose of the flash-forward and the crosscutting between Elizabeth preparing for the speech and the gathered clergymen? What did we learn or feel about her because of this technique?

2. How did Elizabeth's contrasting costumes help to establish her character?

3. What was the turning point in this scene? When was she able to gain control in the situation? How was this change conveyed cinematically?

See Figure 21 for a sampling of what my students found as they looked at the characterizations of Elizabeth and Odysseus (we happened to be studying *The Odyssey* as I was writing this section). Notice that, as with previous activities, the characters have little in common but the analytical skills needed for decoding a text and a film are quite similar. I always ask students to write a thesis statement about these characters, and maybe even a full paragraph if I'm feeling mean.

Considerations	Elizabeth in *Elizabeth*	Odysseus in *The Odyssey* (Book 9)
Behavior	Puts head in hands in practice. Tries to shout over men.	Tricked the Kyklops into calling him "Nohbdy." Kept his men cheered with "battle talk."
Appearance	Dressed in white at first, pure. Changes into bright red.	Strong enough to drive the six-foot spike deep into the eye. [A follow-up question here might address why students commented on Elizabeth's appearance but Odysseus's prowess.]
Dialogue	Practicing her lines. Makes jokes at the men. Talks about "her people."	He told Kyklops that he, Odysseus, blinded him.
Feelings	Scared, frustrated and nervous, then strong and confident.	He is confident to his men, but also prideful when he told Kyklops his real name.
Director's/ Writer's Craft	High-angle shot of her, light shining down from heaven?	Descriptions of Odysseus's bragging and dislike for the Kyklops.

Write a thesis statement about each of the two characters:

1. Elizabeth is very uncomfortable as Queen, but she is getting the hang of it.
2. Odysseus is a cunning man who is too full of himself.

Figure 21. Considering characterization.

The Remains of the Day (James Ivory, 1993)

1:27:17–1:30:20

To put this scene in context: Mr. Stevens, played by Anthony Hopkins, is a butler who has spent much of his life in the service of the lord of the mansion. Recently, a housekeeper, Miss Kenton, played by Emma Thompson, has come to work in the house, and they appear to have become infatuated with each other, though neither has acted on it in any way. As this scene begins, Mr. Stevens is nodding off in his very low-key-lit study while reading a book when Miss Kenton enters, bringing flowers she has picked for him. When she asks him what he is reading, he dodges her question with other questions and retreats to the far corner of his study, as she continues to tease him slightly about the book, while steadily advancing toward him. When she asks if it is a "racy" book, he responds evasively with, "Do you think such books are to be found on his lordship's shelves?" When she has him backed up into the corner, the camera uses a series of very tight, claustrophobic medium shots, and the nondiegetic music has begun, signaling that this might just be the moment when they reveal their feelings to each other. They are so close to each other; the scene, now by the window, has become a little brighter. He holds the book over his heart, while his other hand appears to be almost touching her hair (see Figure 22). As she literally pries the book from him, we hear the exaggerated diegetic sound of fingers being pulled off; maybe his heart needs prying? But, then the music stops, and Miss Kenton declares that the book is not scandalous at all, but just a "sentimental old love story." Embarrassed either by his nearly exposed emotions or by his reading choices, Mr. Stevens asks her to leave and not to disturb his private time. The scene ends with a beautiful, low-key long shot of Mr. Stevens still in his corner, unmoving, but looking out where she has left.

Questions to Consider

1. What does Mr. Stevens reveal about his character through his word choice, movements, and gestures?
2. How does lighting and the nondiegetic sound affect the characterization of Mr. Stevens?
3. How do the framing choices (close-ups, longs shots, etc.) reveal emotion in this scene?

Henry V (Kenneth Branagh, 1989)

1:30:00–1:33:07

The war between the English and the French in this film version of Shakespeare's history play has not been going well for the English, who have successfully invaded France but now face a much stronger, larger, and well-rested force in the upcoming climactic battle. The nondiegetic sound is of a slow, mournful, drumlike dirge, though this could also be the diegetic sound of the French military drummers looming above. Spirits are low, and the men and officers alike are grumbling, bordering on treason, when King Henry overhears them and delivers his "Crispin's Day Speech" in order to rally his troops. As he begins, he is in the center, on the men's level, but as he continues he moves to a makeshift platform above the gathered crowd. The nondiegetic music changes radically to a very light, then swelling and rousing, melody (notice his

Figure 22. This shot tells the whole story of Mr. Stevens's moment of choice in *The Remains of the Day*: the book over his heart and his hand nearly touching Miss Kenton.

position within the frame in the shot in Figure 23). Throughout his speech, we cut from medium shots of Henry back to shots of the soldiers who are clearly being deeply affected by his words. When Henry says that "we few, we happy few" are the only ones to share in this glorious victory, we the audience see the only close-up in the scene. The music reaches its crescendo just as Henry shouts "upon St. Crispin's Day" and we see long shots of the men shouting and pumping their fists in the air. I've seen this scene countless times, and it's goose bump city every time.

Questions to Consider

1. What does the director do to distinguish Henry from the rest of the soldiers in this scene? Think mise-en-scène.
2. Think back on the words Henry uses to rouse his men. What makes this speech so persuasive? What are his best arguments?
3. What does the director do to make us feel like we are the soldiers caught up in the action?

After your students have analyzed how one (or more) of these film clips uses characterization, they will easily be able to transfer those same elements to a short passage from a novel or story that you are reading in class. When these two activities are done either in the same class period or shortly after each other, you will be surprised at how much the students are able to transfer to the written text. They seem to become almost hyperaware of the littlest detail.

The most successful culminating activity that I've done is to ask students to write a thesis statement for each of the characters—from the films and from the stories. Then, they can select one character about which to write a paragraph that explains and supports the thesis statement. Or, they could be asked to write a paragraph comparing the characters in a written and a visual text. Again, the idea is mainly to practice with film, but the real payoff comes when students can analyze literature as well as they do film.

Setting

When we ask our students to analyze the setting of a written text, too often we get merely a description of the weather, the time period, the time of day, or what the place looks like. These are all fine and necessary, but surely we want our students to go a bit further by focusing on how this setting can affect character, theme, and/or plot. So of course I'm going to suggest, "Hey, let's look at some films and their settings,

Figure 23. All eyes are on the king in *Henry V.* The framing, angle, and costume choices add to the characterization.

and then let's look at some written texts." These films illustrate how setting can play an important role in terms of the story and can even act almost as a symbol for the themes of the rest of the film. Horror films can work extremely well for making this point, though many of them contain violence that might not be acceptable in some classrooms.

Falling Down (Joel Schumacher, 1992, rated R)

0:00:00–0:04:40

This is not a great film, and, in fact, many critics complained that it presented negative stereotypes of just about every cultural group in America, but the opening sequence is just a perfect example of how setting can affect a character, and the first four minutes do not contain anything that might be construed as offensive. I have to thank a student of mine, Forrester Karr, for bringing this clip to my attention. After the initial credits, the first image we see is an extreme close-up of a mouth with drops of sweat above the lips; the camera moves up to the nose, then the eye, still in the extreme close-up. There is no sound, except for the very quiet, diegetic sound of someone slowly breathing in and out. When the camera pulls back, we see a man in a short-sleeved white shirt and tie, played by Michael Douglas, sitting in his car stuck in traffic on the highway. The camera then leaves the man, and the nondiegetic sound slowly fades in: a high-pitched, almost mechanical sound. The diegetic sound grows, gradually, to include car horns, radios, kids yelling, and car engines as the camera moves across the crowded and claustrophobic highway. So far, we have had only one long, uninterrupted take, and, when we finally get our first cut, we are back inside the car with the original man. It's hot, his air-conditioning apparently does not work, and his window will not roll down. Now we are getting a lot of cuts, many of them eye-line matches, as the man takes in everything around him: women putting on makeup, people yelling into their cell phones, children laughing, bumper stickers with conflicting messages, and the lines of traffic ahead in the distance. The man is always framed in a close-up, and the nondiegetic sound adds a steady bass drumbeat that quickens with each cut. A fly lands on his neck, and he swats at it repeatedly and viciously; he becomes enraged in his unsuccessful attempts to kill it. The camera seems to be unstable and jerky when it frames him, and we are now back to the extreme close-up of the start. The cuts are coming very rapidly now, the framing has become more extreme, and the nondiegetic and diegetic sounds are flooding the car. His eyes dart to scan the images around him. The music and the cuts stop only after the man opens his door and gets out of his car. With no cuts, and framed in a long shot, the man walks away from his car and runs toward the roadside, leaving it all behind him.

Questions to Consider

1. How do the changing rhythm and pace of the editing affect your response to the setting?
2. Discuss the different framing choices that the director uses in this scene and their effect on us.
3. Describe the mise-en-scène of this sequence and how various elements in the setting affect the man's decision to leave.

Sunset Boulevard (Billy Wilder, 1950)

0:11:40–0:14:50

Down-on-his-luck Hollywood screenwriter Joe Gillis, played by William Holden, is running away from some debt collectors when he makes a quick turn into the driveway of what he says in a voice-over is probably an abandoned house. When he pulls his car into the garage, he notices an old car up on blocks with three inches of dust and several tarps covering it. He approaches the house, which he calls "a great big white elephant of a place," and then he comments that "a neglected house gets an unhappy look; this one had it in spades." Finally we get to see what he has been describing: in a long shot, he is in the center, surrounded by an overgrown garden, an immense unkempt house, and dying palm trees. Just as he makes a reference to Miss Havisham's house and her wedding dress from *Great Expectations,* a female voice calls out "You there!" We follow Gillis's gaze as the camera dollies toward a window covered with broken bamboo shades, and we can tell that someone is behind the shades but we cannot see anyone per se. Suddenly a door opens and a man dressed as a servant appears and motions for Gillis to come into the house. He hesitates briefly, and, even though everything he has seen and thought should send him running away, he goes to the door. Fool. Curtly instructed by the servant, played by Erich von Stroheim, to wipe his feet, Joe enters the house as the nondiegetic sound takes a noticeably suspenseful turn. Clearly the servant has mistaken Gillis for someone else, though this does not stop Gillis from going up the stairs when told to, and the last line of the scene is the servant's cryptic statement, "If you need help with the coffin, call me." Gillis again hesitates briefly, but the house has, in some way, drawn him in despite all the warning signs. A cut to a medium shot of a confused and slightly nervous Gillis ends this sequence. He is inside, and he will never really leave again.

Questions to Consider

1. How was the house itself used to create suspense in this scene?
2. What contrasting images or ideas did you notice in this scene? What is the effect of those contrasts?
3. (After briefly explaining the *Great Expectations* reference to your students . . .) How does the mention of Miss Havisham act as foreshadowing? What in the mise-en-scène reinforces this fore-shadowing?

Vertigo (Alfred Hitchcock, 1959)

0:57:34–1:01:37

In this very odd but great Hitchcock film, James Stewart plays Scottie, a detective hired to watch over his friend's wife Madeleine, played by Kim Novak, who appears to be suicidal and possessed by the ghost of a relative of hers who apparently committed suicide herself at just about Madeleine's age. Scottie has fallen in love with her, and she appears to be interested in him, though obviously she's got some other issues going on. In this scene, Madeleine takes Scottie out for a drive in Northern California, and they end up in a forest of great sequoia trees. The first shot inside the forest is an extreme long shot, so much so that, on the first few viewings, you may not even see the two standing there, and the next shot is another long shot, but at least we can make them out, though they are dwarfed by one massive tree alongside them. When Scottie asks Madeleine what she is thinking, she says that she can only think about all the people who have died while the trees lived, and she says, "I don't like it." Throughout this scene there are so many long shots that the two characters get lost, especially Scottie, whose dark suit blends into the background. In contrast, Madeleine stands out in her white coat, and the focus is so soft that when she goes behind and among the trees, she seems like a ghost appearing and disappearing and floating around. When she and Scottie look at a cross section of one the huge trees, its rings labeled with significant dates, Madeleine points to a date near 1880 and says, "Here I was born," and moving her finger slightly, "here I died." She walks away and seems to have disappeared again, but when Scottie catches up to her, she says, "Take me away from here . . . somewhere in the light." The last shot in the forest is, appropriately, a long shot with Scottie barely visible, Madeleine floating beside him, and the trees towering over them. Obviously, this forest is representative of fate or some larger force dominating and controlling them (those who have seen the film know that it is a little of both). If you like, you might show the very next scene, which takes place "in the light," on a rocky beach next to a dead tree stump. When Scottie and Madeleine finally kiss at the end of the scene, waves crash up against the rocks next to the two doomed lovers. This is no *From Here to Eternity,* waves-on-the-beach kiss; this is a violent, overwhelming love that won't be controlled.

Questions to Consider

1. How do the surroundings seem to affect both Madeleine's and Scottie's moods?

2. Why so many long shots? Doesn't something get lost with so few close-ups? What is gained?

3. What elements in this scene seem to act as foreshadowing?

Next, you should look at a short story or novel that your class is reading in order to examine the setting and its effect on characters. Edgar Allan Poe is always great for setting. Think again about the beginning of "The Fall of the House of Usher," where the house itself causes the narrator's spirit to be pervaded by "a sense of insufferable gloom." I also love to use anything by Barbara Kingsolver, though she is not usually so dramatic.

To help your students refine their thinking about the effect of setting in film and in printed texts, you might use a chart similar to the one shown in Figure 24 (this chart is the result of a classroom pairing of *Falling Down* and Barbara Kingsolver's *Animal Dreams*). As the figure indicates, after students have made notes about how the settings affect character and/or audience, a great additional activity is to ask them to draw one of the settings they saw in the film as well as one from the printed text you are reading. Obviously, this is another reading strategy, but it also helps with analysis because the students need specific details to support their drawings. In my experience, students are more willing and equipped to pick up on such considerations about setting after they have been exposed to analyzing their effects in film.

Point of View

As with the analysis of setting, when we study point of view our students often do not go beyond merely identifying a particular type of narration. They can easily identify whether the narrator is first-person, third person limited, or third-person omniscient. But obviously we would like for them to be able to explain how the choice of narration

Considerations	*Falling Down*, directed by Joel Schumacher	*Animal Dreams* by Barbara Kingsolver
Details of Setting	Hot, crowded highway, fly buzzing, car window doesn't go down, no air-conditioning, kids screaming, horns honking.	Geraniums, potted flowers, light pouring in, flowering vines, a fairy-tale bed.
Effect on Character(s)	Man gets claustrophobic, overheated. He gets very agitated and stressed out. He gives up waiting and leaves it all behind him.	The narrator says that she could fall down and sleep for a hundred years in a house like this. Everything makes her feel comfortable.
Director's/Writer's Craft	Director gives a lot of extreme close-ups and quick cuts showing the man's frustration. The music builds up faster and faster.	She uses a lot of descriptions of flowers and other plants that make the place seem like a nice place to be. She has the character go around opening up every drawer so we expect some kind of mystery or secret.

Now, choose one of these two settings and, on the back of this sheet, draw a picture of the most important aspects of the setting.

Figure 24. Considering setting.

affects what we, the audience, know or feel about a subject. Can the narrator be trusted? Do we know more or less than the characters at a certain point, and why? Do we sympathize with certain characters because of the type of narration? These are the kinds of questions we can help answer by using film as a way to introduce the analysis of point of view.

Before we examine specific films for point of view, we ought to explore in general terms how point of view is expressed through film and where this may overlap with point of view in literature. There is no exact parallel (like those we saw in considering setting and characterization) between point of view in film and point of view in literature, but Cynthia Lucia, a high school teacher of English and film, as well as a professor at New York University, taught me about what is called "focalization," which is very similar to point of view in literature. The term "focalization" offers a way to describe film shots by identifying the point of view behind those shots. There are three such classifications: subjective, authorial, and neutral.

Subjective

This is a type of shot—or series of shots—that align us clearly with one character's point of view. It is normally established through the use of an eye-line match and it generally shows us only what the character is seeing or what he or she is able to see. Imagine, for example, that we see a man hunting lions in the middle of a jungle. We hear a sound and we see him looking around, then we cut to what he sees: something rustling in the bushes. Then maybe we cut back to his face tensing up, and then we cut back to the lion leaping out. The lion is rushing directly toward the hunter, toward the camera, and thus toward us. We see what he sees and feel what he feels. This might be closest to a first-person kind of narration where the narrator is an actual character in the story and we see it through his or her eyes. This means, of course, that sometimes we do not get certain information, since the character, too, does not have it.

Authorial

In this type of shot, the view cannot be attributed to any character within the film and thus it is a way for the director (the "author" of the film) to give information directly to the audience without also giving it to one of the characters. Back to our lion hunter: We hear the same sound and see the man looking around, but this time we do not cut to his point of view; instead, the camera dollies around behind him and shows us a huge, ferocious lion waiting in the bushes. Cut back to the man unaware of the lion's presence. In a long shot now, we see the hunter standing there with his gun as the lion is bearing down on him from behind. We, the audience, have information that the character does not. This type of information, though, does not always have to be communicated only through the framing of the shot. Authorial information could come in the form of lighting that comments on a character's inner state of mind, or music that signals that a big shark is coming or that a killer is on the way to the character's shower. This type of shot and this method of conveying information might best be described as third-person omniscient because the audience gets the details directly without their being filtered through a character. This does not mean, however, that this narrator is to be trusted anymore than a first-person narrator, only that its source is different.

Neutral

When we were looking at framing, angles, and lighting, we found that the medium shot, the eye-level angle, and the even lighting are all relatively neutral in the sense that, by themselves, they do not automatically carry any significant meaning. In terms of focalization, most shots in a film will be characterized as "neutral" because not every shot can be subjective (i.e., taking a single character's point of view) or authorial (i.e., readily identifiable as coming straight from the director). So, if our lion hunter story were going to be filmed neutrally, we might see the hunter, then cut to the lion, and then cut back to the man as he runs away from the lion and the camera. We might not get an eye-line match, nor might we see some dramatic low angle emphasizing the power of that lion. Maybe this point of view is closest to a third-person narrator who observes but does not comment, intrude, or get inside characters' thoughts. This may not fit exactly with the strictest definitions, and we ought not to force it.

These are very rough descriptions (see Figure 25 for visual representations), and whether a shot is subjective, neutral, or authorial is often subject to interpretation and debate. In addition, the connections between film and literature narration should not be made too explicitly, since the purpose of this chapter is not to find strict parallels between the two mediums but to see how certain point-of-view choices affect the viewer or reader. It is important to note that, within a given scene, the focalization may switch several times between subjective, authorial, and neutral, depending on what the director intends. Thus the most interesting aspect of considering focalization in a film is to identify when it changes and why the director makes this choice. I know of only one major studio attempt at making a film using only subjective shots (the dreadful *Lady in the Lake,* where all the characters talked directly and rather awkwardly into the camera). Thus most films, unlike most works of literature, switch frequently between these types of focalization in order to achieve desired effects. This shifting is what makes using film to teach point-of-view so successful: we can see clearly how the changes in point of view can communicate so much information so quickly.

Notorious (Alfred Hitchcock, 1941)

1:25:00–1:28:30

Cynthia Lucia used this clip in her classes to introduce focalization because it illustrates so clearly the different types of shots and their

Subjective

Shot #1   Shot #2   Shot #3

We see the hunter looking, we see the lion in the bushes through his POV, and then we see his reaction.

Authorial

Shot #1   Shot #2   Shot #3

The high angle long shot in #1 emphasizes the precarious position the hunter is in, and shots #2 and #3 give the audience information that the hunter does not have.

Neutral

Shot #1   Shot #2   Shot #3

We do not see anything through the hunter's perspective, nor do we see any dramatic angles, lighting, or framing that might suggest an authorial shot.

Figure 25. Point of view in film.

effects. Ingrid Bergman plays Alicia, a reluctant American spy who marries Alexander, a suspected Nazi, for the sole purpose of getting information to assist the Allies. Alexander, played by Claude Rains, and his mother have figured out Alicia's deceit and have started to poison her slowly by putting arsenic in her coffee. The scene begins with a close-up of the coffee cup as the mother pours, and the camera remains focused in a close-up on the cup. This first shot, obviously, is authorial because Hitchcock is saying to us, the audience, "Hey, pay attention to the cup, the cup!" while Alicia, unaware, accepts the cup. If this bit had been shot neutrally, we probably would have seen the mother, framed in a medium shot, merely carrying the cup across the room. As the scene continues the three of them and a guest have a conversation about Alicia's not feeling well, and most of this interaction is shot neutrally, until Hitchcock cuts to a medium shot of Alicia, with the coffee cup in the front of the frame in a close-up. In this type of authorial framing, the cup looks even larger than Alicia; Hitchcock is again saying, "Did you miss the cup last time? If so, look at it now! It's huge!" We also catch authorial glances from the mother and husband as Alicia drinks from the cup. At one point, however, when the guest accidentally reaches for the tainted cup, both the mother and husband nearly jump out of their seats to stop him. Now we get a series of subjective shots from Alicia's point of view (see Figure 26 for a shot where we are moving toward her point of view). She looks at them, then at the cup, then to each of them, zooming in on their guilty faces. As she stands up, she is unsteady and we see her husband and his mother through her drugged eyes: they are out of focus, they turn into shadows, and the sound is distorted. She leaves the room, goes into the hallway, and falls down on the hard floor. The scene ends with a high-angle (authorial) shot of her lying on the ground amid a chessboard-like tile pattern, as Hitchcock implicitly asks, Could this be checkmate? (If you think I'm reading too much into this, see the still in Figure 27.)

Questions to Consider

1. What did Hitchcock gain by having the audience in on the coffee cup before Alicia realized it?

2. Why did he suddenly switch to the series of subjective shots? How would the effect have been different if he had shot the whole scene neutrally?

3. Is nondiegetic music always authorial? How could it sometimes be subjective? What about in this case?

Figure 26. The beginning of the shift to a subjective perspective in *Notorious*.

Figure 27. Back to an authorial point of view in *Notorious*. The high angle and chessboard floor demonstrate Alicia's weakness and entrapment.

Jaws (Steven Spielberg, 1975)

0:57:37–1:03:06

Like Hitchcock, Spielberg is a master manipulator, which I think of as a compliment. As we saw in the previous clips dealing with point of view, this one from *Jaws* contains various types of focalization for the purpose of either giving information to the audience or keeping details hidden from it. Despite several shark attacks, the beaches are back open on the Fourth of July in Amity, which the mayor reminds us means "Friendship," after local fishers have caught what most people assume was the killer shark. The scene begins with a series of neutral shots that show people in the water and continues with back-and-forth cuts between the water, the shore, and the men in boats with rifles keeping watch. Everything seems fine, until the camera switches to its water-level shot, which throughout the film has been a signal of attack. Next, we see several underwater shots of the swimmers from below; these can be either subjective shots from the shark's point of view or authorial shots used as foreshadowing (you will find out which at the end of the clip). Just after the mayor of the town pronounces the beach safe for a TV news reporter, we get two authorial shots of a dorsal fin sticking out of the water that slips behind several swimmers and one of the shark watchers, unnoticed. Two close-ups of frightened faces and two screams signal a switch to subjective point-of-view shots positioned with the swimmers as they frantically scramble for the shore; the chaos of the evacuation is captured through these handheld, jerky, quick-cutting subjective shots. But where's the shark? Is it behind us? Has it attacked anyone? There are no authorial shots to let us know: we are the swimmers, unknowing and fearful. After the panic subsides, we learn that the fin was just a hoax by two young boys, so those underwater shots we saw earlier were clearly authorial, tension-creating shots, and not subjective shots from the point of view of the shark, which was not around at that time. A bit later, when a woman starts yelling about a shark, we think nothing of it, thinking that it's still part of the hoax, until we see another authorial shot of a huge fin moving quickly toward a small boat with four boys. The boys and a man have their backs to the coming shark, though we can see it plain as day. When the shark attacks the man, we see it through the eyes of one of the boys, who then becomes frozen with shock. We now see the boy from that water-level point of view, which is clearly established as the shark's view, as the shark rushes by him. The scene ends when the boy's father and others take him out of the water.

Questions to Consider

1. What information did the director give to the audience and what did he conceal? What was the effect of these choices?

2. Why does most of this scene contain only diegetic sound? When does the nondiegetic music begin? Why then?

3. If you had to insert one authorial shot into this scene, where would you put it and why? If you were to add a subjective shot, where would it go? For what effect?

Psycho (Alfred Hitchcock, 1960)

0:58:19–0:59:47

After you have introduced the concepts of focalization with the previous clips, this one can be used to explore more closely the real power of choosing one type of focalization over another. Just prior to this scene, Marion Crane, our only main character of the film so far, was brutally murdered while taking a shower, and Norman, a lonely hotel manager who had dinner with her that night, discovers the body and begins to clean up the mess and dispose of her body because he assumes that his mother killed her. So, in this scene, Norman, played by Anthony Perkins, puts her body in the trunk of her car and takes it down to a conveniently located swamp, into which he pushes her car. Now we see a series of subjective shots: Norman looking at the car nervously, hoping it sinks. Cut to the car sinking. Back and forth. There is only the diegetic sound of the car sinking—bubbling sounds as the swamp takes her. Back and forth. Then, suddenly, nothing; the sound stops. Shots again of Norman, then subjective shots of the car *not* sinking, then back quickly to Norman, nervous. It's gotten stuck, we think. He looks around. Back to the car, stopped and sticking out of the swamp in plain view. Back to Norman, and then we hear the sound of the sinking again. Finally we see another subjective shot of the car vanishing into the swamp. Norman visibly relaxes and a small smile escapes. I urge you to watch this scene to see just how Hitchcock uses the subjective shots to get us to root for Norman in this scene. Every time I see this scene, I always get tense when the car stops and I am relieved when it starts to sink. But I know that I should not feel this way; our main character is dead and in the back of the trunk. If the car sinks, Norman will get away with (at least) the covering up of a murder, and yet still I am relieved, just like he is, at the end. Why? Hitchcock makes us look through Norman's eyes with those subjective shots, and, consequently, we feel how he feels. Sure, it's manipulative, but that's also just good filmmaking—and good storytelling.

Questions to Consider

1. Why do you think Hitchcock felt it necessary to make us feel for Norman at this point in the film?

2. How does the lack of nondiegetic sound add to the suspensefulness of this scene?

3. If you wanted to add an authorial shot to this scene, what would it be, and what purpose would it serve?

A Christmas Story (Bob [Benjamin] Clark, 1983)

1:08:34–1:10:40

This is a very funny sequence that contains a few wonderfully filmed subjective shots. Ralphie is waiting in line to see a department store Santa in order to ask him about getting a Red Ryder BB Gun for Christmas. His mother insists that he'd just shoot his eye out, so Ralphie has no choice but to see the man himself, though he says that he really doesn't believe in Santa anymore. This sequence starts just as his younger brother is put onto Santa's lap, but he gets scared and starts screaming before he can make his request. So now it's Ralphie's turn, and we get a series of subjective shots showing his own fear of Santa, whose chair is perched far above the floor. First we get a shot from Ralphie's POV as he is violently whipped around and swung onto Santa, who looks distorted and quite disgusting this close up. In the subjective shots, Santa and his helpers are terrifying and rude, while in the neutral shots they appear much closer to normal. His fear causes Ralphie to forget what he wanted for Christmas, so when Santa suggests a football and Ralphie nods in agreement, he is slung onto a slide to take him back down. At just the last moment, he remembers his wish, stops his slide, and blurts out his request for the BB gun. After Santa tells him, "You'll shoot your eye out, kid," we switch to a subjective shot of Santa and his helper, in a low angle, of course, as Santa raises his boot and puts it right in Ralphie's face, sending him down the slide.

Questions to Consider

1. Besides being from Ralphie's point of view, the subjective shots also seemed to be distorted, as if filmed from inside a fishbowl. Why were they shot that way?

2. Most of the humor seems to come from the point-of-view shots; how would this scene have been different if it had been filmed neutrally?

3. What subjective shots from Santa's point of view would have been interesting or funny to see?

After you have examined not only how film uses point of view, but also why a director might choose one point of view over another, you should turn to pieces of literature that have distinct narration. While most traditional fiction does not suddenly change point of view types within the same story, a lot of fiction uses subtle changes in focus where we seem to be getting multiple perspectives. One of my favorite stories to use with this exercise is Ernest Hemingway's "The Short Happy Life of Francis Macomber," in which the focus switches often between several of the characters, including a lion. After examining point of view in film, the students will be better equipped to explain why differing kinds of narration are used for differing effects.

Symbol

When we read with our students, we often point out all the relevant and important symbols in a story or novel. I have heard myself saying things like, "This twig, of course, is a symbol of his inability to love." Really, I said that once. We assume that students cannot pick up on a symbol on the first read-through, and that may be true, since, for a symbol to be truly a symbol, it must be repeated throughout a work, though maybe students also have difficulty picking out symbols because they do not understand the purpose or the function of symbols. An AP teacher from San Diego, Mike Ayers, gave me a great definition of a symbol: "It is what it is and something more." In other words, that twig *is* a twig, but it is also representative of something greater. So we need to help students see how artists use various techniques to get the audience to recognize that something is, in fact, a symbol. To the rescue, once again, is, wait, wait, don't tell me: watching some film clips? Film works so well for symbols, as in these below, because directors can be so obvious in saying, "Hey, look at this! This is important!" by lighting it or framing it a particular way. But of course Hawthorne is quite obvious at times; I mean, come on, a big red "A"? The analysis of symbols works best when studied over the course of the entire work, but I think that each of these film clips stands on its own in its use of symbols. As we watch these clips, I have students keep a sort of symbol tally sheet listing the recurring references. I give also give them blank tally sheets to use in tracking symbols in written texts we are studying (see sample in Figure 28).

Film and Literary Analysis:
Symbol Tally Sheet

As you watch each of the following film clips, keep track of the number of times that you see or hear a reference to the object that is acting as a symbol. Afterwards, identify the literal and make a guess about the possible metaphorical meanings of that symbol.

Film Title	Object	# of Visual References	# of Dialogue References	Literal Meaning	Metaphorical Meanings
Psycho	Birds	✓✓✓✓✓	✓✓✓✓	Norman likes to stuff birds for a hobby.	Birds can be caged or they can be free; birds can be tame or they can be dangerous.
The Man Who Shot Liberty Valance	Cactus Rose	✓✓✓	✓✓✓✓	The cactus rose grows in the desert and is a gift from Tom to Hallie.	The rose manages to grow despite the harsh conditions. It is pretty in a rough way, but is not quite so as a "real" rose.
The Piano	Piano	✓✓✓✓✓✓ ✓✓✓✓	✓✓✓✓✓✓✓ ✓	The piano is Ada's most prized possession.	The piano is an extension of her voice; it is how she communicates with others and herself.

Now as we read the following short story, keep track of the references to the following that may be acting as symbols.

Story Title	Object	# of Direct References	# of Indirect References	Literal Meaning	Metaphorical Meaning
"Young Goodman Brown"	Faith	✓✓✓✓	✓✓	The name of Brown's wife.	He is losing his religious faith.
	Snake/ Serpent	✓✓	✓✓✓✓✓✓	He sees one in the woods. The staff is shaped like one.	Temptation, sin, and desire.
	Forest	✓✓✓✓	✓✓	The dark place where he meets them.	The unknown part of himself and others.

Figure 28. Symbol tally sheet for several films and one short story.

Psycho (Alfred Hitchcock, 1960)

0:34:26–0:44:08

Marion Crane, played by Janet Leigh, has stolen money from her employer and, in running away, has ended up at the hotel of amateur taxidermist and full-time mama's boy Norman Bates, played by Anthony Perkins. He has brought her some food to eat and he suggests that they eat in his parlor (said the spider to the . . .). As she looks around, the very first thing she notices is a huge, stuffed owl with wings spread wide as if caught in midflight. She notices other stuffed birds on the walls and on the tables around the room. "You eat like a bird," he says to her, and he's actually right because Marion, as she pecks at a piece of bread throughout the scene, holds her hand oddly twisted to resemble a bird's claw. I swear I'm not making this up; she really does look like one. Her last name of course continues the bird references. Norman says that he likes to stuff birds because they are kind of "passive to begin with," though the birds of prey all around appear to have been anything but passive when they were alive—and even *less* so now. Their conversation continues about how everyone can fall into "private traps," and, when Marion mentions his mother, the camera angle and framing change dramatically so that we now see Norman in a low angle from the side, with the light clearly playing off of only one side of his face, and, more significant for our purposes here, there are now two huge birds with outstretched wings looming over both sides of his head. When she gently suggests that he put his mother into an institution, the framing changes again, but with another, smaller bird next to him, as he says that his mother is as harmless as one of these stuffed birds. (If you've seen the movie, feel free to laugh; if you haven't, put this down and rent it now, unless you haven't bought this book yet, in which case, keep reading—the movie will still be there!) After Marion leaves the parlor, Norman can hear her moving around next door, and, as he spies on her through a hole in the wall, the birds again fill the screen around him (see Figure 29). Hitchcock layers so many references to birds through the dialogue, the mise-en-scène, and the performances that we must be in the realm of symbols. If students can recognize how an artist uses his or her techniques to present symbols, the real fun comes in trying to decipher them.

Questions to Consider

> 1. How did Hitchcock's framing choices lead you to see that the birds were somehow important?

Figure 29. See, I'm not making this stuff up: Norman and the bird imagery in a publicity still from *Psycho*.

2. Think back on what Norman said about the private traps people get into. How does this relate to the bird symbol?

3. How do the birds seem to represent Norman, and how do they seem to represent Marion as well?

The Man Who Shot Liberty Valance (John Ford, 1962)

0:37:45–0:41:09

This classic Western uses the repeated symbol of a desert cactus rose to represent the political conflicts between the civilized East and the developing West, as well as the personal conflicts between two men and the woman who loves them both (sounds like a cheap romance novel, huh?). James Stewart plays Ranse Stoddard, a lawyer from the East who has come to bring justice to this backward region, John Wayne plays Tom Doniphon, a rugged rancher who lives by the Western code that might makes right, and Vera Miles plays Hallie, a waitress who is drawn to Ranse's educated ways but also attracted to Tom's strength. Hallie opens this scene by announcing that Ranse is going to "learn her" to read and write, and, when he corrects her usage, he stands behind her and puts his hands on both her shoulders. They are like this when Tom enters, who glares at how close they are to each other. Tom gives Hallie a present of a cactus rose, a thin cactus with three tiny white rose blossoms sticking out of it. As Hallie declares its beauty, Ranse glances at it dismissively. Tom looks and then reads aloud a sign that Ranse has painted for the law office that he plans to open. Tom warns him that if he does, he'll have to defend it with a gun, adding that Ranse "ain't exactly the type." On his way to the dining room, Tom flirts with Hallie, telling her that her face is as pretty as that cactus rose. Tom sits down to eat with a newspaper editor, and, when he cannot take his eyes off Hallie, the editor asks whether wedding bells are coming soon for Tom. The very next shot is of Pompey, Tom's assistant, planting the cactus rose right outside the kitchen door. Hallie stares at it and calls Ranse over to ask if it isn't the prettiest thing he ever did see. A light nondiegetic tune has slowly faded in as they look at it together, and Ranse seems slightly bemused when he asks her, "Have you ever seen a *real* rose?" The tune grows louder when she replies, "No, but maybe someday." The scene ends when she is called back to work. This clip is not so glaringly obvious as the birds in *Psycho,* but it clearly demonstrates again how a filmmaker can scatter references to an object throughout a scene so that the object is almost forced to take on a greater significance.

Questions to Consider

1. Trace how each of the three main characters feels about the cactus rose. What does that say about their conflicts?

2. What was Ranse implying by asking about a *real* rose?

3. After looking only at this clip, with which character do you most sympathize? Why this one?

4. How do you think the symbol of the cactus rose might play out in the rest of this film?

The Piano (Jane Campion, 1993, rated R)

0:00:00–0:13:51

With the title alone, students should easily recognize that the director is using the piano as a symbol, but, like the other examples, this one uses many different means to make the significance of the symbol clear. The first line of the film states, "The voice you hear is not my speaking voice, but my mind's voice." The woman, Ada, played by Holly Hunter, tells us that she does not know why but that she has not spoken since she was six years old, and she says that her father has arranged for her to be married to a man in New Zealand, whom she has not yet met. Signs of her and her daughter's trip are everywhere. Walking amid the packing crates, she tells us that she is not really silent because she has her piano, which she strokes gently before sitting down and playing a beautifully dramatic and flowing tune. As soon as a woman walks into the room, however, Ada stops suddenly and stares harshly at her. The piano is already established as an extension of her voice and her personality. The next scenes are of a very rough landing of a small ship on a rocky and deserted coast. The piano crate is off-loaded and Ada guides and directs the operation until they have placed it exactly where she wants it. After the sailors leave, we see a series of long shots, showing Ada and her daughter alone, with their possessions scattered all over the beach, waiting for her fiancé to arrive. She breaks off a piece of the crate holding the piano, just enough space for her to reach one hand inside to play a few notes as her daughter sleeps on her lap. After spending the night on the beach, they are awakened by her husband, played by Sam Neill, and some men he has brought with him to carry her things the long distance to his home. When he says that the piano cannot be taken now, she offers to leave everything else instead. He refuses. Next we see a long shot over her shoulder of the piano, which is well below her, left behind on the barren beach by itself. The take is very long and the nondiegetic music sounds similar to the song she was playing earlier. From there the director cuts to several seconds of a close-up of Ada looking down toward the piano, and the scene concludes with a long shot of mother and daughter standing on the hill looking very ill-equipped and out of place in their new home.

Questions to Consider

1. Describe the several ways in which the director made the piano take on a greater importance than simply a musical instrument?

2. How could the nondiegetic music of the final shot be seen as internal diegetic? What effect does this have?

3. Besides being a voice for Ada, what else do you think the piano signifies for her?

So, now you ought to look for stories, poems, or a novel in which symbols play an important role. I mentioned Hawthorne earlier, but Shirley Jackson, Flannery O'Connor, and Edgar Allan Poe can also be counted on for great use of symbols. The most important thing we can do as we turn to examining symbols in literature is focus on what the author does to help us recognize the importance of a symbol. Does the writer repeat the image or describe it in a striking manner? Does it seem to be an extension of a character in some way? Again, the idea is to put the students in charge, so I won't ever again have to say anything about what that twig symbolizes: when these strategies work, *they'll* tell *me* about it.

Irony

Probably the most difficult literary device to teach is irony because it is so difficult even for us English teachers to grasp sometimes. Perhaps irony is like the famous Supreme Court definition of pornography: "I don't know what it is, but I know it when I see it." No, please, I am not about to suggest renting one of *those* films to show irony to your students (though I have *heard* that there is plenty of irony in them). Rather, film has a way of putting conflicting images together in such a way that the students can easily recognize that the director may be commenting on the irony of the situation. Or, as my good friend and colleague Kevin Cline patiently explained to me, irony in film (and literature) is all about "puncturing the expectations of the viewer" (or reader). In other words, what you expect to see is undercut either by what you hear or by a contrasting visual image, so that the result is the mirror image of your expectations. So, we're not talking about surprise or twist endings in a film, though they often might be ironic, nor are we talking about satire, which is often similar to irony. The best examples of irony in film are the ones hinting that the meaning intended by the director (or writer) is the exact opposite of what he or she appears to be presenting.

Good Morning, Vietnam (Barry Levinson, 1987, rated R for no good reason)

1:28:02–1:33:00

A simple and straightforward example of irony comes just past the midpoint of this comedy/drama about an American radio announcer in Vietnam during the war. It begins with the DJ, played by Robin Williams, putting on a record, and we then see a montage of life in Vietnam during the war. As scenes slowly unfold before us—bombs being dropped, soldiers marching across muddy fields, civilians running away, people being arrested in the streets—we hear Louis Armstrong's "What a Wonderful World." It is the clear contrast between the visual image and the sound that leads the viewer to recognize fully the ironic statement of the director. As Armstrong sings, "I see friends shaking hands," for example, we see instead a group of street protesters being beaten by police. He sings, "I see skies of blue and clouds of white," just as a cloud is formed by an explosion behind a group of farmers. This visual is the direct opposite of the expectations one would have for the song, and vice versa. It is the absurdity of war and the difficulties involved in trying to communicate with others that the director illustrates so well through his use of irony. It really is a textbook example.

Questions to Consider

1. Play the Armstrong song before looking at the clip. If you do not have the song on tape or CD, play the scene from the movie with the TV turned backwards. Ask the students to imagine visual pictures that might correspond to the song.

2. Play the film clip with the sound turned down. Ask your students about their feelings and what they might expect to hear if the sound were turned on.

3. Now, play the clip with sound and ask your students how the scene is different with these conflicting ideas. Ask them if they can define irony from this activity.

Blue Velvet **(David Lynch, 1986, rated R for very good reasons)**
0:03:22–0:05:34

Warning: As noted above, this film is rated R and it contains excessive
violence, language, and other elements that are not even close to being
appropriate for the high school classroom, and if the film's opening were
not such a perfect example of irony, I would not have used it. I would
not even consider using any other part of this film in my classroom.

After the entire opening credit sequence, we see a perfect blue
sky with birds chirping, and lovely red roses are blowing lightly against
a white picket fence, while the 1950s-styled song "Blue Velvet" plays
on the nondiegetic soundtrack. A bright red fire truck with a Dalma-
tian and a waving firefighter rolls by slowly, and a single-file line of
schoolchildren crosses the quiet street with the assistance of a uniformed
crossing guard. We draw closer to one house and cut to the back, where
a man is watering the yard and, inside, a woman sips tea while watching television. At this point, you may wish to stop the tape and ask students about what they have seen. Obviously, this is a town that is too
perfect, too quaint. So are we in satire? A spoof, perhaps, of America,
Mom, and apple pie? But wait—keep watching. The first sign that we
are in a state of irony comes when we see that the woman is watching
some type of crime drama in the middle of the day that shows a close-
up of a hand holding a huge gun. Then, back outside, the man watering his lawn is having some difficulty with his hose, which has gotten
wrapped around a bush. As he pulls and yanks, we cut rapidly between
the bush, the water faucet, and the man. It seems to be building to some
type of climax, when the man suddenly grabs his neck and falls to the
ground thrashing in pain. Meanwhile, the same drippy "Blue Velvet"
song has been playing continuously and no one has come to the man's
aid in this quietly perfect town. Slowly the camera follows the spray-
ing water across, and eventually it moves through the grass he had been
watering, shot in extreme close-up. The song fades away to be replaced
by some unidentifiable (diegetic?) gnashing and crunching sounds. The
camera continues to move through the grass, and the ground itself, until
we finally can identify those sounds: insects—horrible and violent—are
fighting and tearing at each other while their sounds obliterate everything else. Cut immediately then to a beautiful billboard sign declaring, "Welcome to Lumberton." Obviously, we have conflicting, mirror-
like images of this town: it is a perfect place so long as you do not look

too closely, because then you might see the ugliness that lies beneath. The irony of safety, security, and neighborhoods is exposed by showing us the town's inhuman foundations. All this is done without a single piece of dialogue.

Questions to Consider

1. What was your first sign that all is not well in Lumberton?
2. After a second viewing, what is your impression of the song "Blue Velvet"? Why do you think it was selected?
3. What predictions do you have about the rest of the film? What leads you to make these predictions?

Citizen Kane (Orson Welles, 1941)

Times noted below

As discussed earlier, Welles tried to tell much of his story and the characters' relationships simply by the use of lighting and angles. In particular, he used lighting to comment on the irony of certain situations. For example, at one point early on in the film (0:37:10–0:38:44) we see Kane as a young man preparing to put out the very first issue of the newspaper that will one day make him famous. But right now, he is nervous and feels that something is missing. He decides to print his "Declaration of Principles," which state, among other things, that his newspaper will always tell the news honestly. Now, everything that we know about lighting would lead us to expect that as the character talks about honesty, he would be shot in high key and probably with front lighting. But just as Kane prepares to sign, his face is entirely shrouded in darkness. Irony as foreshadowing since his newspaper, as it turns out, will not always tell the truth. In a sequence earlier in the film (0:17:33), Thompson, the reporter assigned to discover the meaning of Kane's dying word, "Rosebud," enters a room where he will read a diary that he hopes will give him his answer. The room is dark except for a single, bright shaft of light from above that illuminates the book. The audience's expectation upon seeing this lighting choice is clear: this book has the answer to the mystery because light is knowledge. Unfortunately, by the end of the scene, Thompson still is no closer to his goal: irony as red herring. But, Welles pulls a sort of double irony on us because that diary did in fact show us Rosebud, though we and Thompson were unaware of it until the end of the film. (Did you notice how cleverly I constructed the preceding sentence so as not to reveal the mystery of Rosebud? Hurry up and see the film—I cannot be trusted to keep doing this!)

Questions to Consider

1. What makes us expect certain things to happen because of how a scene is lit? Can you think of examples from other films you have seen?

2. How are irony and foreshadowing similar in these scenes?

3. How does sound contribute to the irony of these scenes?

Edward Scissorhands (Tim Burton, 1990)

0:07:20–0:15:30

After the opening titles and a brief introduction, this sequence begins with the local "Avon lady," Peg, played by Dianne Wiest, going door-to-door in her perfect, cookie-cutter, pastel-colored neighborhood, getting turned down every time. As she gets into her car, she readjusts the side-view mirror and suddenly we see a huge, towering castle behind her. With nothing else, presumably, to lose Peg decides to try her luck there. From this point on, just about everything in this scene contains irony. One would not expect an Avon rep to come knocking on the door of a castle that is clearly meant to resemble the haunted mansions of the Frankenstein movies; for that matter, one would not expect such a place to exist just at the end of the neighborhood's cul-de-sac. But the irony continues because the castle, and its lone occupant, Edward, played by Johnny Depp, continually contradict everything that we might have expected with the setting and the music. Is this a horror film? Then why are the castle grounds so well manicured? (See Figure 30 for a shot of Peg in the garden.) Why is the creature so sweet and helpless? These contrasting images are repeated throughout the sequence, especially in the last shot, which shows this supposed monster, Edward, happily riding in Peg's car through the neighborhood to her home. The film and the actors will be familiar to many of your students, so this might be a great place to really confirm their understanding of irony.

Questions to Consider

1. What are the various contradictory images in this scene? What is the effect of these contradictions?

2. How is the audience supposed to feel during this scene, and how do those feelings change?

3. How are the music and costume choices also ironic?

Just as in each of the other sections, now is the time to think about stories that employ a good deal of irony. The students will have a good working definition and several good examples that will prepare them

Figure 30. The conflicting images and expectations create irony in *Edward Scissorhands*.

for the irony of writers such as Chekhov, O. Henry, and Poe. At this point, students should be better equipped to articulate the irony of a piece of literature beyond saying that it's a twist ending or some type of sarcasm. Thus we can take back our definition of irony, which pop singer Alanis Morissette robbed from us when she recorded a song called "Ironic," in which she listed several examples of what she thought were irony, such as a "fly in your Chardonnay" or "rain on your wedding day." For years, kids have parroted these horrible examples to me. The irony master, my colleague Kevin Cline, pointed out that the wedding day instance would, of course, be ironic if the bride or groom were a meteorologist. But as it stands, perhaps you can use this song after the film clips to show what irony is *not*.

A couple of final thoughts about using film and literature occurred to me while putting this project together, and I thought I might as well throw them out there. On the literary analysis side, I think that you could make up some wonderful exercises that focus specifically on word choice and syntax in film and literature; I imagine a series of short clips with some of the most famous lines from film, such as "Here's looking at you, kid," or "Frankly, my dear, I don't give a damn." Why were they so effective? Why are they still known today? I also think tone could be separated from setting as another topic for analysis. I would love to see a few clips that really get at how tone is the author/director's attitude toward his or her subject. How does lighting, music, or framing reveal the tone of a piece? This is fertile ground for analysis at the AP level. Another rich possibility would be to use film clips to help students understand how foreshadowing gets used, and to what effect.

On a different note, I think the visual image is also a great tool for teaching critical thinking skills. A teacher friend of mine from Maryland, Rick Robb, uses commercials to help his students understand how the media manipulates its viewers. You can carry a lot of your film knowledge over not only to TV ads but to print ads as well, since they use many of the same techniques. Deconstructing political advertisements would be an extremely worthwhile analytical exercise.

A final thought is to use film not only to analyze literature but also to create it. Think about the improvement in your students' fiction writing that might occur if you use these film clips as examples of good characterization, setting, dialogue, and so on. I could imagine exercises where students might be asked to continue a scene, write an ending, imagine a new setting, develop an appropriate symbol, rewrite from a different point of view—or anything else that would be helpful for creative writing.

I could see all of these ideas working nicely, but since I had enough trouble with the ones I've already described, I'll leave the new ones for someone else to write about; just make sure I get a copy of it, please.

4 Teaching a Complete Film

Whenever I decide to show an entire film to one of my classes, I try very hard to examine my motives about what I want to accomplish during this time. Am I looking for a break from my planning and teaching? Is it right before a holiday, when the kids have turned into human equivalents of pinballs? I will fully admit to answering yes to both of these questions during desperate times. I want to nominate for sainthood any teacher who doesn't admit this—or strap him or her to a polygraph.

But, since we have been talking seriously about the use of film in the classroom, we ought to think about the appropriateness of teaching a complete movie, which can take a week or more of class time. Perhaps you want to introduce students to film technique and narrative structure, maybe you want to examine the variety of film genres, such as western, horror, film noir, or others (for an excellent resource on teaching genre, see *Reel Conversations,* described in the Books about Film in the Classroom section of Appendix C); or maybe you want to explore further a theme that you have studied in various print texts. All of these seem to be perfectly fine reasons to show an entire film to your class. I am not in any way trying to discourage the use of complete films, but I always want to have a purpose in mind whenever I get that call from a parent whose child has said that all we do is watch movies in class. Having a clear purpose in mind makes these conversations go much easier, and, as a result, the discussion of each film that I suggest below starts with a rationale that you can either use as is or adapt to create your own justification.

I also suggest questions or activities for you to consider before your class starts watching the film. In the same way that we use prereading strategies with a written text, these questions can help your students consider the themes, subjects, actors, or directors they will encounter.

When I first started teaching entire films, I made a mistake, tried to fix it, and ended up doing worse than before. I was teaching Alfred Hitchcock's *Rear Window,* and I jumped up every minute or so, paused the video, and said things like, "Did you see that great shot? What do you think that means?" A little more film, another jump, another pause, and another inane comment from Golden (I actually once said, "Look—there's a bird. Hitchcock made another movie called *The Birds*"). After about five days of this—not getting more than an hour into the film—I was exhausted from the exercise and my students were dizzy and completely without the flow and sequence of the film. The next year, I decided that I would do better and give the students the real experience of watching cinema. I played the film straight through without a break and without a peep from me, which was *very* difficult. It was also very stupid, because the students slipped into their typically passive film-in-school mode and missed many key elements. Relating this to a novel, how often do you ask students to read *A Tale of Two Cities* straight through, without any comment from you? So, like the slow learner I am, I realized by the third year that I should create a schedule that balanced the students' need to have a somewhat genuine cinematic experience with my need to be able to point out and discuss significant details.

Since I have found that I can be quiet for just about twenty-five minutes without hurting myself or others, I suggest breaking the film into what I call "Viewing Days" that include roughly that amount of time for watching the film and taking notes, with the remainder of the class time spent on discussion and on re-viewing particular key scenes. For each Viewing Day, I also list a few sample discussion questions that can be used to prompt analytical response from your students—or that can just be ignored like most discussion questions found in textbooks.

You will also find some closing questions and activities that can wrap up your study of each film. Most of the films here will take about five to six class days, including pre- and post-viewing activities on a fifty-minute period; adjust as you need for a block schedule, though I still advise against a straight-through viewing, even if you can do it all on one day.

One final word about what students should be doing during the viewing. For all of the viewings described in previous chapters of this book, students in my classes were always asked to be engaged in some kind of writing or responding during the clip. I suggest that this occurs when watching entire films as well. For older high school students, I use a note-taking form (see the form titled Film Viewing Notes in Appendix B) that was adapted from an activity in Teasley and Wilder's *Reel Conversations*. It asks students to note significant elements of the film in three categories (theatrical, literary, and cinematic). I have had good luck with this form, which also includes a part for them to work on immediately after the day's viewing while I am busily trying to find that key sequence that I want them to view again. The form also includes a place for students to reflect on what they have seen of the film so far, and I usually have them do this part for homework. For younger students, I usually provide a little more specific guidance about looking for particular elements (e.g., a close-up, instances of low-key lighting, or a particular theme). There is a sample of this form (titled Note-Taking Form) in Appendix B as well.

Many of the films in this section are well known, and quite possibly your students have already seen some of them, but don't let that keep you from teaching them. Students will see the benefit of watching it more than once if they are asked to look at the film in different ways than they have before, which is why I recommend that you make sure, before you teach a complete film, to introduce at least some of the film terms discussed in Chapter 1. As with the other chapters of the book, use this section as a list of suggestions that might work well for you, but I am sure that, as you read, you'll think of many more that will work just as well or better for you.

The films discussed in this section, by grade recommendation, are:

- Middle School: *The Lion King* and *E.T. the Extra-Terrestrial*
- Grade 9: *Crooklyn* and *King of the Hill*
- Grade 10: *Life Is Beautiful, Frankenstein,* and *Bride of Frankenstein*
- Grade 11: *Rocky* and *Smoke Signals*
- Grade 12: *Cyrano de Bergerac* and *Elizabeth*

The Lion King

1994, Rated G, Directed by Rob Minkoff and Roger Allers

Rationale

I know, I know. A cartoon? Disney? But I must be honest: I was a sucker for this film even before I really noticed the fact that, even though it's a cartoon, it is virtually a textbook for cinematic technique. The framing, angles, music, and editing are handled as effectively as in any Alfred Hitchcock movie. It also works well as an introduction to film and literary analysis, since the characters, conflicts, and themes are obvious but also meaty enough to support extended writings and discussions (remember, it's really *Hamlet* for tots).

Previewing

Most of your students have already seen this film, though, being in middle and high school, they may be reluctant to admit it in front of their friends. But I still suggest a few opening questions and activities.

- Genre: Start by asking your students what Disney movies they have seen. What do most Disney films have in common? What do you like or not like about them? Why are they so popular? Also, a couple of quick facts to share about *The Lion King*: it was the thirty-second animated Disney movie, the first without any human characters, and the first based on a wholly original story.
- Character: What responsibilities would be involved in being a king? What would be the good side of it, and what would be the downside?
- Theme: This film discusses—and sings about—"The Circle of Life." What does this concept mean, and how do you see it in your daily lives?

Viewing Day #1: 0:00:00–0:25:05 (about 25 minutes)

- Begins with: opening credits
- Ends with: Simba and Mufasa under the stars

Things to Notice

The establishing shots of the plains (see Key Sequence below) set the tone, theme, and setting of the "natural order" of life. Scar is often in shadows and has a scraggly black mane in contrast to Mufasa's (and later Simba's) golden mane. As Simba walks behind his father, his feet are too small for Mufasa's footprints (don't you just love obvious symbolism to be able to point out to kids?). Also notice the wonderful scene of Simba and Mufasa talking under the stars, with the camera pulling back to a long shot to show them dwarfed by the stars that Mufasa says represent great kings who look down on them.

Key Sequence: 0:01:54–0:04:02

This is when Simba is presented to the gathered animals. Great low angles and high-key lighting represent not only the power but also the respect shown by all the animals. This is the perfect and natural order of things shown by the crosscutting to all the animals bowing as the song "The Circle of Life" is heard. This scene is important to highlight because it demonstrates the order that will be thrown into chaos by Scar's usurpation and because it will be echoed twice at the end of the film.

Discussion Questions

1. What does the song "I Just Can't Wait to Be King" reveal about Simba's character?

2. How do the directors communicate the shift in tone when Simba and Nula go to the graveyard? How do they create suspense for the audience and show the fear of the two young lions?

3. Every two-year-old who watches this film immediately knows that Scar is the bad guy. How do the directors show this so quickly to the audience?

Viewing Day #2: 0:25:05–0:57:20 (about 32 minutes)

- Begins with: the hyenas talking about Mufasa
- Ends with: Simba and Nula recognizing each other

Things to Notice

Watch for the amazing lighting, framing, and angles used during the song that Scar sings with the hyenas. The whole scene is clearly designed to echo Hitler's Nuremberg rally: shafts of light, leader high on podium, gleaming troops marching below. It's a beautiful nightmare and very effective. Be sure to point out the stampede scene and Mufasa's death (see Key Sequence section just below) and the long shot of Simba's running away. When Scar takes over, we see a wasteland in low-key lighting with bones and filth everywhere. In exile, Simba meets new friends and adopts the "Hakuna Matata" philosophy, that is, "no worries," as a shot of the young Simba dissolves into a shot of an older Simba, showing time passing. His childhood friend Nula finds him at the end of this day's viewing.

Key Sequence: 0:32:00–0:35:46

This is the stampede, which is shot with a series of crosscuts between the helpless Simba (shown from high angles) and Mufasa on his way to the rescue. There are very short takes and quick zooms into the action. Notice too the cuts to reaction shots of Simba as his father falls to his death.

Discussion Questions

1. What did the directors do to make the scene of Mufasa's death so powerful for the audience?

2. What is Scar like as a leader? What has changed since he has taken over? How is the setting itself different and why?

3. Summarize the philosophy of Hakuna Matata. What are the positive aspects of it for Simba and the negative aspects of it as a philosophy of life?

Viewing Day #3: 0:57:21–1:22:54 (about 25 minutes)

- Begins with: Timon starting to sing
- Ends with: the closing credits

Things to Notice

The pressures of responsibility overwhelm the appeal of Hakuna Matata for Simba when Rafiki asks him, "Who *are* you?" and reminds him that he is his father's son. As during his earlier departure, a long shot of Simba shows him surrounded by the waste of Scar's rule. It is interesting that, though Simba defeats Scar, he does not kill him—the hyenas do it for him. But after the final battle, normalcy is returned (see Key Sequence below), and, to demonstrate the circle of life theme again, a young lion cub, born to Simba, is presented to the gathered animals.

Key Sequence: 1:19:16–1:22:08

Simba defeats Scar, and the fires that had been burning are put out by a soothing rain that also quenches the parched land and signals to the animals that it is safe again to return. The music swells as Simba ascends Pride Rock, and we see him in a low angle, rightfully restored on his throne.

Discussion Questions

1. Nula's insistence on Simba returning did not work. What finally led Simba to realize that he had to go back?

2. What went wrong with Scar's rule? Why was he not able to govern effectively? Would it have been different if Scar had a son?

3. How do we know that everything is back to normal at the end? What clues do we have?

Closing Questions/Activities

1. The story of *The Lion King* is an original one, though it has some similarities to Shakespeare's *Hamlet*. Watch one of the many film versions that have been made of *Hamlet* and discuss the similarities and differences between it and *The Lion King*.

2. Taking the point of view of Simba as an adult, write a letter to Timon, thanking him for sharing his Hakuna Matata philosophy but explaining why it might not be the best way to live one's life. Give evidence to support your position.

3. The animals in this film seem to have mainly human characteristics, though with some animal traits. After conducting
   some research on lions and other African animals, describe
   how this story might be different if the animals operated instead as they do in nature.

4. This film presents the form of government known as "monarchy." What are the pros and cons of this type of government as
   it exists in the real world with human beings? How might the
   view of monarchy presented in the film seem different if it were
   made with live human actors rather than animated animals?

E.T. the Extra-Terrestrial

1982, Rated PG, Directed by Steven Spielberg

Rationale

A modern and enduring fairy tale, this film is both cinematically rich
and simple enough in its story and characterization for middle or el-
ementary school students to be able to analyze. It would be a great beginning to the study of the language of film because Spielberg is quite
straightforward in his use of framing, music, and lighting.

Previewing

1. Director: Before starting this film, I would ask my students
   what Spielberg films they have already seen. It's quite a list:
   *Close Encounters, Jaws, Raiders of the Lost Ark, Hook, Jurassic Park,
   Schindler's List, Amistad.* What do these films have in common?

2. Story: What films do you know that deal with extraterrestri-
   als? Describe or draw pictures of some of the aliens in these
   films. How do you imagine someone or something from another planet might look or act?

3. Genre: This movie has sometimes been called a fairy tale. What
   plot or character elements are usually included in a fairy tale?
   How do they normally end?

Viewing Day #1: 0:00:00–0:25:20 (about 25 minutes)

- Begins with: opening credits
- Ends with: the menacing key-wearing man in the forest find-
  ing the candy

Things to Notice

The opening section is told mostly from the point of view of the alien creature (see Key Sequence below), and we see the men only in low-key light

and from the waist down. In several sequences that follow, Spielberg builds the suspense and shows Elliot's fear through music, low-key lighting, crosscutting, and especially the use of the close-up on Elliot's face. But notice how we and Elliot become more accustomed to looking at E.T., so he quickly stops being a source of fear.

Key Sequence: 0:00:00–0:07:51

The opening sequence establishes the E.T. character very quickly by showing us that he has been left behind because he was being too inquisitive, looking up at the huge trees that dwarf him and the town in the valley that interests him, and we hear his childlike screams when being pursued. This sequence also establishes a point of view that remains mostly consistent through the film: we see adults from a child's perspective.

Discussion Questions

1. Why did Spielberg choose to start his film with images of E.T. instead of starting with Elliot and his family? What feelings do you have after that opening scene? How did Spielberg help you to feel this way?

2. What do we already know about Elliot and his family? Why do you think this information is important?

3. How does the director make the scenes before Elliot meets E.T. suspenseful?

Viewing Day #2: 0:25:10–0:55:35 (about 30 minutes)

- Begins with: Elliot playing sick
- Ends with: the classic line "E.T. phone home"

Things to Notice

We begin to see that there is some kind of connection between Elliot and E.T. Also, we see that E.T. has the power to heal when he makes the flowers regrow; these particular flowers will act as a foreshadowing device, hinting at E.T.'s declining health. When Elliot goes to school, where we still see adults from the waist down, there is further evidence of his connection with E.T.: as E.T., hiding at Elliot's home, drinks beer, Elliot also gets drunk. An interesting element of the story is that Elliot's mother appears to be so busy or caught up in the day-to-day world that she cannot see E.T., though he walks right by her several times.

Key Sequence: 0:27:10–0:30:11

This is a simple but sweet scene about Elliot's first attempts at communication with E.T. It is interesting also because of the childlike things that Elliot wants to teach him about: toys, candy, and pets. Think about what an adult might try to teach an alien and you can see the genuineness of Elliot. The scene is also shot with the light of the window behind them, so we see only their silhouettes in a soft focus, which emphasizes the tenderness of their budding relationship.

Discussion Questions

1. Typically, whenever a character sees E.T. for the first time or sees him do something spectacular, Spielberg first shows us the person's reaction and only *then* shows us what the character is seeing. Why do you think he does this, and what is the effect?

2. Why do we usually see adults only from the waist down, and why is it that Elliot's mother cannot seem to see E.T. even though he's right in front of her? What is Spielberg saying about adults?

3. Why does Elliot let the frogs loose, and what does this say about him as a character and about his treatment of E.T.?

Viewing Day #3: 0:55:30–1:19:37 (about 24 minutes)

- Begins with: Elliot and his brother in the garage
- Ends with: scientists coming in with space suits

Things to Notice

The crosscut to the men listening in on Elliot's conversation with his brother shows us that the menace hinted at in the beginning of the film is growing nearer. E.T. and Elliot listen to his mother reading the story of Peter Pan to his sister (see Key Sequence below). Those flowers we saw earlier are losing petals. You may want to point out that the lighting has become decidedly low-key and the mood somber after the Halloween excursion in the woods. When the scientists come into the house, they are made to look much more threatening and frightening in their space suits than E.T. ever did. Finally we see the face of the key-wearing man.

Key Sequence: 0:57:33–0:59:22

Another gentle scene between E.T. and Elliot occurs when they are hiding in the closet and listening to Elliot's mother read the story of Peter

Pan. The lighting is again soft and low-key, with very quiet and slow music. The picture of Mom reading a bedtime story suggests an idealized portrait of a family, and Elliot completes it by putting his arm around E.T., just after his mother reads the line about believing in fairies.

Discussion Questions

1. What hints have we had all along that E.T. and Elliot are somehow connected and that they are dying?

2. How is the audience supposed to feel about the government agents? What did Spielberg do to get us to feel this way?

3. What similarities are there between this story and the story of Peter Pan? Why was the Peter Pan story included here?

4. Why does Elliot seem so possessive about E.T.? Why is he insistent that they do not tell his mother?

Viewing Day #4: 1:19:37–1:50:00 (about 31 minutes)

- Begins with: E.T. and Elliot in hospital beds
- Ends with: closing credits

Things to Notice

The camera perspective has shifted noticeably, as we no longer see the adults only from the waist down. The key-wearing man and Elliot are also connected insofar as each believes that E.T. came to him personally. The flowers continue to die, and E.T. appears to have passed away, though of course he has not, which is hinted at by the regrowing of the flowers. The race to return E.T. to his ship pits the children against the adults again, and the crosscutting is played for humor and suspense, but this time the kids get to win over the adults. As the good-byes are given at the base of E.T.'s ship, Spielberg gives numerous close-ups and reaction shots. E.T. tells Elliot that he will "be right here" and touches Elliot's head.

Key Sequence: 1:43:20–1:48:00

I am writing this as I watch this good-bye scene for like the hundredth time in my life, and I look over at my wife, and she is bawling though she tries to hide it. She hides it, I think, because she knows it's pretty manipulative, but when you look at what Spielberg does—close-ups, reaction shots, lights on each face, swelling music, and E.T.'s "ouch" line as he points toward his heart—it's easy to be swept up. So I suggest reviewing this scene to examine particularly how the director makes us feel the emotion of this parting.

Discussion Questions

1. Why did the perspective change in this day's viewing so that we now see the adults in normal framing? What is Spielberg saying about the change in power?

2. How does Spielberg make us feel the emotion of the good-bye scene? Describe the use of framing and music, as well as the performances.

3. There are several small references to Elliot's absent father. What role do you think that played in Elliot's reaction to E.T.? What hints does Spielberg give that the key-wearing man may play a role in Elliot's life?

Closing Questions/Activities

1. Write a series of diary entries from Elliot's point of view to trace his thoughts and feelings from the day before he met E.T. to the day after E.T. left.

2. People love to talk about a sequel for *E.T.* Write a plot for a story that has E.T. return to Earth when Elliot is thirty years old. What would happen?

3. Watch another film that has an alien who comes to Earth. Compare this alien with E.T., focusing on how this alien was treated by humans and, in turn, how the alien treated them.

Crooklyn

1994, Rated PG-13, Directed by Spike Lee

Rationale

Spike Lee is one of America's most original, daring, and controversial directors. He focuses on subjects and themes that most Hollywood filmmakers wouldn't know what to do with even if they did touch them with a ten-foot pole. Many of Lee's films seek to counter racial stereotypes of African American life by creating characters who are full, real, and alive. He and his movies are lightning rods for every sort of attack from African Americans as well as Whites, but at least he is out there hitting nerves like good filmmakers should do. Unfortunately many of his films are rated R for violence, sexual situations, and especially vulgarity. Personally I would love to teach his brilliant *Do the Right Thing*, but my community might not be so comfortable with the profanity. So all this brings us to *Crooklyn*, a very good, though maybe not great, Spike Lee film. It is not a politically charged film but a rather endearing coming-of-age story, told from the perspective of a young African American girl.

The uniqueness of the film's perspective and the universalness of its theme should justify its inclusion in a ninth-grade class, but cinematically, and especially musically, Lee has recreated time and place (1970s Brooklyn) so effectively that it also works very well for film study.

Previewing

1. Plot: Ask students to write down a list of memorable incidents that happened to them when they were younger. Tell them not to worry if the event seems insignificant or if they cannot remember it well. Ask them to focus on family, friends, trips taken, or any event they remember in some detail. After they have lists of ten to twenty events, have them try to put the events into chronological order and to write down as many details (sights, sounds, smells) of those events as they can recall. Finally, have them put it all together in an episodic narrative or, for those who are artistically inclined, have them draw a series of pictures.

2. Music: Have students generate another list of their five favorite songs. Then ask them to choose one of these songs that might go along with one of the events they described in the narrative above and to describe how it would fit as if it were a music video of that event from their lives. The song should become a sort of soundtrack for that event in their lives.

3. Setting: Before the first viewing day, show the first five minutes of the opening titles sequence, until the kids go inside for dinner. What does this neighborhood look like? What is the time of year? How does the song fit in with the pictures on-screen? (The chorus is "People make the world go 'round.") If you are not on the East Coast, I have also found it important to help students with the geography of New York City, especially the location and history of Brooklyn.

4. Setting (part two): Have students draw pictures of their own neighborhoods in a style similar to that of the shots they saw in the opening section of the film. They should label where certain people live, what games get played where, and the important locations in their area. How are theirs similar to and different from what they saw of Spike Lee's Brooklyn?

Viewing Day #1: 0:00:00–0:30:00 (30 minutes)

- Begins with: opening titles (even if you showed them earlier)
- Ends with: neighbor's arrest

Things to Notice

The tender but chaotic family life is shown by the quick takes, fast-moving camera, and overlapping dialogue. You will notice quickly that the pace of the movie changes all the time: a very busy scene is typically followed by a quiet and slow scene. When Lee films the drug sniffers (that's Spike Lee as one of them), he reverses the image and shows them floating upside down, clearly showing the ill effects of drug use and how out-of-norm it is in the neighborhood. We also see that the father is the bringer of treats to the family.

Key Sequence: 0:12:55–0:14:28

After the craziness of the night before, Lee shows us an overhead shot of Troy in the morning. The camera moves slowly and catches her just waking up, with light music in the background which acts as her own theme song throughout the film. For the first time, we see just a single person in a scene. The mood continues as she goes downstairs to find her mother in her favorite chair and they share a quiet moment (see the top photo in Figure 31); matching close-ups establish their close relationship and resemblance. They are the only women in a family overrun by men.

Discussion Questions

1. What is the tone and mood of this movie so far? What helps to create this atmosphere?

2. What are some of the conflicts that seem to be developing? What do you think this movie is going to be about? Why?

3. Watching this film so far, you could say that nothing has happened. How is the plot of this film different from most? Why do you think the writers and director chose to tell their story this way?

4. What similarities or differences have you seen between this film and your own life and family? Think about dinner time, dealing with siblings and parents, and your neighborhood.

Viewing Day #2: 0:30:00–1:07:00 (37 minutes)

- Begins with: kids watching *The Partridge Family*
- Ends with: family arriving at relatives' house

Things to Notice

When the parents and kids get into the big fight, Lee cuts quickly back and forth while the up-tempo song "I'll Take You There" plays on the soundtrack. The audience is left somewhat unsure about whether to laugh or cry during the scene. Troy has another quiet scene alone with a parent, this time with her father on the steps outside. In framing, tone,

Figure 31. Troy is the peacemaker and the image of her mother in *Crooklyn*.

and music, it mirrors the earlier scene with her mother (see the bottom photo in Figure 31).

Key Sequence: 0:54:36–0:56:11

This is Troy's nightmare scene, and it begins with overhead shots of her bedroom that are identical to those in yesterday's Key Sequence, but this time the lighting is low-key and the music is fast and jagged. In bed, Troy is writhing around, almost like she is running in place. And in her dream, which has a dark blue, off-focus tint to it, she is running away from the drug sniffers. They catch her and force her to sniff, and she floats away, as the song ("Time Has Come Today") also fades away.

Discussion Questions

1. Who is the main character of this story? How do you know? Why did the director take so long to establish her as the main character?

2. Music plays an important part in the family's life and in the film. What songs stuck out for you and why? What effect do they have on you?

3. What elements in this film seem to date it to the 1970s? What aspects still seem similar to their counterparts today?

4. What do you think Troy's dream signifies, and why did Lee film it that way?

Viewing Day #3: 1:07:00–1:29:00 (22 minutes)

- Begins with: family going into the house
- Ends with: Troy being picked up at the airport

Things to Notice

Do not adjust your television sets: Lee intentionally distorts the frame when the family goes inside the house by using an anamorphic lens, which squeezes the images together. Obviously this approach is used to demonstrate Troy's feelings of unease outside of Brooklyn, and the effect is just as disorienting for the viewer. While much of what she sees is new for Troy, especially when she has to have her hair straightened, she brings her "Crooklyn" spirit for games and mischief, which seems to influence her cousin. When Troy receives a letter from her mother, the words come to life in the form of images from the neighborhood, which are not filmed with the distortion. Troy's perspective returns to normal in terms of the frame as she gets off the plane back home.

Key Sequence: 1:21:00–1:22:53

This is a short but wonderfully effective scene tucked into the sequence where Troy reads the letter from her mother. It starts with the father's concert, then flashes forward to the party afterward, and finally back to the concert to reveal that the audience is small and that Clinton, the eldest, is not there. When Clinton comes home and announces that the Knicks won the championship, which he went to instead of his father's concert, it is clear that the father is hurt, but still generous to his son, who probably won't be able to watch a game again without some guilt. It's a nice scene to show how a great performance, by Delroy Lindo as the father, good writing, and an effective use of close-ups can make a simple scene powerful.

Discussion Questions

1. Why did the director, Spike Lee, choose to distort the image when depicting the time Troy spends outside of Brooklyn? What is the effect on you as the viewer? Do you get used to it? Does Troy?

2. While this is primarily Troy's story, what other conflicts are going on in this family?

3. What new things was Troy exposed to while she was in the South? How do you think these experiences will affect her later on?

4. Much seems to be made of Troy's hair in this film. Why did her Southern aunt straighten it? What did her other aunt think of her hair when she returned to Brooklyn? What other references to hair have you seen so far?

Viewing Day #4: 1:29:00–1:49:35 (about 20 minutes)

- Begins with: the hospital
- Ends with: the *Soul Train* dance and the credits

Things to Notice

Both mother and daughter have new hair when they see each other in the hospital. While her mother is sick, Troy is the only child not crying. During and after the funeral the chorus of the song is "Someday things are going to be easier." Troy is alone at the reception after the funeral, and her big brother Clinton does his first nice thing in the movie by sitting down next to her and taking her hand. Immediately after this, we hear the opening strains of the *Shaft* theme song and Troy goes after the sniffers on their block. Troy begins taking over some of her mother's roles—we see her in her mother's chair combing out her brother's hair—and the film ends with a wonderful shot of the block, with Troy leaning quietly against a fence and gazing peacefully out across her neighborhood. The last song that plays over the credits and scenes from *Soul Train* is a rap song about living in the 1970s and is the only anachronistic song on the soundtrack.

Key Sequence: 1:36:39–1:37:54

I absolutely love this tiny scene. It starts with still, dark, and silent shots of the house that is never quiet and moves to a long, overhead shot of Troy following behind her brothers in a park. We hear the "Hallelujah" song that Troy heard down South and just a tiny voice wondering if they are going to have to dress up for Mommy's funeral. I think the tone, the pace, the song, and the subtle dialogue communicate more real feeling than if Lee had chosen to film a tearful deathbed scene. An interesting question would be why Lee chose not to film Troy's mother dying. I also suggest looking back at the last scenes of Troy taking over the household.

Discussion Questions

1. What has Troy learned from her experiences? In what ways is she just like her mother, and how is she different?
2. How does Troy deal with her grief?
3. Throughout the sequence viewed today, many songs were used to create mood. Describe the effect of one of the songs you heard.
4. What did you notice about the TV programs that they watched? Why do you think Lee chose to end with the characters watching *Soul Train*?

Closing Questions/Activities

1. What does the word "sentimentalized" mean? How is this film a sentimentalized portrait of growing up? How would the film have been different if it had not taken a sentimental approach?
2. Lee and the writers, his two sisters, intentionally wanted this film to be episodic, without a straightforward narrative structure. Why do you think they wanted that approach, and how would the film have been different if the plot had been more structured?
3. Create a scrapbook that Troy might have kept. Put into the book any items that she might have collected (ticket back home,

letter from her mother, etc.) and things that she might have created (diary entries, song lyrics, maps of her block, etc.).

King of the Hill

1993, Rated PG-13, Directed by Steven Soderbergh

Rationale

Ninth-grade classes often focus on coming-of-age stories, and this one fits in so perfectly that it could almost define the genre. It is the story of an imaginative boy's struggles to keep himself and his family afloat during the Great Depression. Soderbergh has such a strong visual and narrative sense that every scene is filled with images and music that contribute to the boy's growing sense of the world. The film received much critical praise but little popular attention when it was released, but it deserves close examination: it is sometimes sentimental and almost always very affecting.

Previewing

1. Time period: The term "Great Depression" is such a part of our American psyche that it's difficult for us to imagine that anyone would be unfamiliar with it. But the enormity of the disaster is still hard to imagine. Discuss such realities as the following (each of which plays an important role in the film):
   - In 1933, nearly sixteen million people were unemployed, which amounts to one-third of the total workforce.
   - The highest unemployment rates were among unskilled workers, young people, and recent immigrants.
   - The New Deal's Works Progress Administration put two million people to work in jobs that ranged from construction, to clerks, to actors.

2. Theme: What is a coming-of-age story? What characteristics do such stories seem to share? Why are they so popular? What other coming-of-age films do you know about?

3. Theme (part two): Think about the most difficult aspects of growing up. What kinds of conflicts do you get into with your parents, teachers, or classmates? What kinds of pressures do you face in growing up?

Viewing Day #1: 0:00:00–0:32:58 (about 33 minutes)

- Begins with: opening credits
- Ends with: Aaron's mother leaving for the sanitarium

Things to Notice

Aaron's character is established through his imagination, though he is not quite as clever as he thinks. Two characters are already set up as foils to Aaron: the police officer and Ben, the bell boy, who locks people out of their hotel rooms when they cannot pay. Often there are Dutch (canted) angles of the Empire Hotel. You may also want to point out a very young Lauryn Hill, years before she became a pop star, as the gum-chewing elevator operator. Your students will think you're very cool for knowing who she is.

Key Sequence: 0:00:06–0:10:02

Aaron meets up with and takes care of his little brother. As the boys run off to the hotel, the music seems magical and nostalgic, and the director plays with the focus, all of which creates a dreamlike quality. Look for the high-angle shot of the boys as they enter the hotel, which signals, in a lot of ways, the end of their play and fun; we never see Aaron quite so happy again. Aaron tells his brother that "all the important things in life can't be taught, you just got to learn it," which is an attitude that will change through the film.

Discussion Questions

1. What are the conflicting moods of this film so far? What does the director do to establish these moods?

2. Do you agree with Aaron's statement that the most important things in life cannot be taught? How do you imagine that this aspect of Aaron's character at this stage might be seen in the rest of the film?

3. Why do you think the director has not shown us the worst aspects of the Depression?

Viewing Day #2: 0:32:58–0:57:39 (about 25 minutes)

- Begins with: Aaron trying to caddy
- Ends with: Aaron receiving his final report card and walking back to the hotel

Things to Notice

Note Aaron's growing sense of the world around him. He starts seeing poverty, prostitution, and the kindness or meanness of people. When his father leaves him, he tells Aaron the story of how he made him stop crying when he was a baby: he threw cold water on him.

Key Sequence: 0:44:03–0:46:00

This is the humorous scene of Aaron trying to drive, but it is also a textbook example of creating excitement and humor through editing, music, and framing. Notice the quick crosscuts to the startled pedestrians, the close-ups and eye-line matches of Aaron, the quick zooms, and the fast-paced music.

Discussion Questions

1. When Aaron delivered the liquor to Mr. Mungo and said he did it as a favor, Mr. Mungo said that "should be a lesson for us all." When have we seen people doing things as favors so far in the film? When have we seen the opposite?

2. How have Aaron's perceptions of the world around him changed or grown? What has caused this development?

3. How has the tone of this film changed? How has the lighting and music changed in accordance?

Viewing Day #3: 0:57:39–1:20:28 (about 23 minutes)

- Begins with: Aaron receiving a letter from the WPA for his father

- Ends with: Aaron running back into his room before Ben locks him out

Things to Notice

More doors are locked and Aaron's own room may be next. There is a Dutch angle on Aaron at the graduation party to demonstrate his distress when he is confronted with his own lies: he also leaves his medal behind. He sees his ex-neighbor Mr. Sandoval in a shantytown and is being more affected by the situation of others, especially when he sees a settlement being broken up across from the hotel. The director plays with the nondiegetic sound when Aaron forges a letter to get his brother sent back.

Key Sequence: 1:01:46–1:04:00

This is Aaron's graduation scene, and the director plays it beautifully. All diegetic sound is dropped out, though we realize that the parents rise when the names of their graduating children are called. We know what is coming up—we know that Aaron will have no one—but, to everyone's surprise, there's his buddy Lester, whistling and causing Aaron to slip. Great low-angle close-ups of Lester, brightly lit, make us feel the relief and joy of having someone there for him.

Discussion Questions

1. What does the director do to make us respond emotionally to two key scenes in today's segment: the graduation scene and the party scene? Think about framing, music, and the actors' performance.

2. How is Aaron more involved in the world around him after the events depicted in today's viewing?

3. Why do you think the character of the prostitute is included?

Viewing Day #4: 1:20:28–1:39:17 (about 19 minutes)

- Begins with: Aaron in his room unable to leave
- End with: closing credits

Things to Notice

When Aaron discovers Mr. Mungo's body, we hear the odd, disorienting, nondiegetic sound as he rushes back to his room, which sounds like blood pumping through his ears. When Sully makes it back home, Aaron teaches him to shoot marbles, despite his earlier attitude about having to learn things for oneself. After his father returns and tells them to just leave everything behind, Aaron refuses, since now he attaches more value to personal possessions than he did before. He also does two more good acts for others: he takes Mr. Sandoval's paints from the storage closet to give to him later, and he takes the keys Ben uses to keep people locked out of their rooms at the hotel. He's learned to appreciate the gesture of giving.

Key Sequence: 1:25:30–1:28:20

This is the very powerful scene when Aaron is feverish and hallucinating. The lighting is low-key and the angles are high and distorted. He sees some images that occurred in reality, but he also dreams of his father's meeting with a prostitute and of his father, not Mr. Mungo, committing suicide. The vision is made up of rapid-fire quick takes and oddly tinted color. When Aaron wakes up, he finally bursts with anger against his father's treatment of him by smashing the candles he tried to sell.

Discussion Questions

1. Why does Aaron refuse to leave the room with his father? What has changed most about Aaron?

2. Interpret Aaron's dream sequence. What images are played out, and what do you think they mean?

3. What do you think the father is thinking at the end of the movie? Why do you think we don't see much of his mother at the end?

4. The cop and Ben were both set up as Aaron's foils. How does he overcome them, and what does this say about him?

Closing Questions/Activities

1. By the end of the film, how has Aaron become the "King of the Hill"? What does this mean to him? How do you think things will be different for him from now on?

2. One of the themes of this film is that in order to survive, you have to be willing to give something to others. How is this philosophy played out in the film, and how does Aaron learn it? How does he teach it?

3. Could the events depicted in the film take place today? What has changed in government, social services, police, education, or other areas that would make Aaron's experience different?

4. Make a chart that tracks Aaron's maturation. Which events taught him which lessons?

5. Taking Aaron's point of view, write a series of thank-you letters to those who helped him. Your letters could be written from an older Aaron who understands what various people did for him.

Life Is Beautiful

1998, Rated PG-13, Directed by Roberto Benigni

Rationale

I must admit that I put off seeing this film for quite awhile: I could not conceive of a romantic comedy set in a Nazi concentration camp. But when I finally saw it, I was immediately swept up by the overriding vision proposed by the title, despite the horrors of the setting. In many school districts, the study of the Holocaust takes place during the tenth-grade year, and this film would be a perfect fit with such print texts as *Night* and *The Diary of Anne Frank,* while being considerably lighter in tone than the often-shown *Schindler's List.* Flora Levin, a teacher from Fulton County, Georgia, shared just such a unit with me a few years back. I think this film also provides an easy way to introduce students to the watching of foreign films, which requires particular kinds of reading and viewing skills.

Previewing

1. Time period: If this film is not being shown as part of a Holocaust unit, then obviously students will need a little bit of background on World War II and the concentration camps. It would
   also be important to discuss Italy's role in the war and its own
   brand of fascism, especially since Guido is mistaken for
   Mussolini in the movie's slapstick opening sequence.

2. Subtitles: If you've ever played a black-and-white film in class,
   you know how students groan, but that is nothing compared
   to showing a subtitled film. So, before the first viewing day, I
   suggest practicing the reading of subtitles. Choose any scene
   from a foreign film (I recommend a high-interest martial arts
   film or a John Woo action film that the kids will enjoy), play a
   few minutes of it, and ask your students only to look at the
   pictures and listen to the sounds. Rewind the scene, play it
   again, and ask them to concentrate only on the words that are
   written below the images. Play the scene one final time as they
   watch for all the elements of the film. Like anything else worthwhile, watching a subtitled film does take practice. Do not,
   however, under any circumstances, consider showing a
   dubbed film; it just is not the same.

Viewing Day #1: 0:00:00–0:35:32 (about 35 minutes)

- Begins with: a scene of fog and a voice-over declaring this story
  to be a fable
- Ends with: Guido getting the dry hat

Things to Notice

This first half of the film is filled with gentle romance as Guido pursues
his "Princess" and gives the actor Benigni opportunities for his trade-
mark slapstick humor, though often the humor hints at the economic
hard times and policies of the fascist regime, such as when he delivers
his "race manifesto" about the Italian belly button. His chance encounters with Dora and his whimsical imagination lay the groundwork for
the rest of the film.

Key Sequence: 0:31:49–0:35:48

On their date that he arranged, Guido rolls out a red carpet for his "princess" and seemingly gets a special key and a dry hat through his magic.
This scene perfectly demonstrates the magical tone of the film and two
important aspects of Guido's character: he is an imaginative dreamer
who always looks on the bright side of the road, and he is able to take

advantage of whatever circumstances he finds himself in. We also get to hear the melody that is repeated throughout the film.

Discussion Questions

1. What are the defining characteristics of Guido's character? How does the actor convey these to the audience?
2. How would you describe the tone or mood of this movie so far? What contributes to it?
3. Is life beautiful so far in this film? Why or why not?
4. What signs have you seen that this will be a film about the Holocaust?

Viewing Day #2: 0:35:32–1:00:54 (about 25 minutes)

- Begins with: Dora's engagement party
- Ends with: Dora getting on the train

Things to Notice

The signs of growing unrest become more apparent in today's viewing. Guido uses a horse that has been painted "Jewish Horse" to rescue Dora from her wedding. There is a nice transition with the garden to show that time has passed. More signs of "No Jews Allowed" appear around town, though Guido tries to shelter his son from their meaning. When Guido is asked to go to the police station for questioning, he mocks the officers for Joshua's benefit by goose-stepping in an exaggerated manner: be sure to highlight this action for your students as it will become important at the film's end.

Key Sequence: 0:57:45–1:00:54

This is when Dora goes to the station after Guido and Joshua have been taken. Notice the looks that the German officer gives her when she decides to board the train voluntarily and the eye-line matches of Guido looking at her through the bars of the train window. This scene, like many of those that follow, plays on the audience's previous knowledge of the Holocaust, so we know, the German knows, and Guido knows exactly what she is sacrificing without anyone having to say it out loud.

Discussion Questions

1. What are the initial signs that Guido is very protective of his son? How does he go about protecting him so far?

2. Describe how music has been used in today's viewing, especially when Guido is taken away by the police officers?

3. How is life still beautiful in today's viewing?

Viewing Day #3: 1:00:54–1:26:40 (about 26 minutes)

- Begins with: The train pulling into the camp
- Ends with: Guido threatening to leave the camp

Things to Notice

This has now become a concentration camp movie, though with much of the same lightness of spirit. Guido sets up the whole camp for his son as a big game with the winners being awarded a real tank (see Figure 32 for a film still showing the boy's reaction). There are many scenes that are reminiscent of other Holocaust films or accounts, including slave labor and "showers" for old people and children. An interesting exchange occurs near the end of the day's viewing when Joshua hears from others that the Nazis make soap and buttons out of Jewish bodies; Guido points outs the absolute ridiculousness of such an idea and gets his young son to admit that nothing so outrageous could possibly occur. The audience knows the horror through the laughter.

Key Sequence: 1:14:41–1:17:45

Like the train imagery, the horrors of the showers at concentration camps are so well known that when Guido insists that Joshua take a shower, we plead along with Joshua not to take one. The remainder of the scene does not show us the people dying in the showers, though we see the old and the young take off their clothes, and later we see the prisoners forced to sort through them.

Discussion Questions

1. How has the tone and mood shifted in this day's viewing? How have the costumes, colors, and music changed to reflect this new mood?

2. Why does Guido set up the game for Joshua? What is he hoping to accomplish?

3. How are the horrific images of the Holocaust used in this movie so far? And how does the director keep these images from greatly altering his tone?

Figure 32. Can a Holocaust film have a shot with this face in it? *Life Is Beautiful* manages to make the boy's expression and the horrors of the concentration camp somehow compatible.

Viewing Day #4: 1:26:0—end (about 27 minutes)

- Begins with: German children playing
- Ends with: closing credits

Things to Notice

Guido learns that the doctor he thought could help them escape is interested only in solving another riddle, which shows again how thoroughly inhumane and insane the Holocaust is. Guido then takes another risk by sending a song out of the window to Dora (see Key Sequence below). When Guido is captured and is being led away, he again goose-steps for the hidden Joshua like he did for him earlier. He is then shot. You may know that it's coming, but it is still quite a shock. He has been in every single scene with us and now he is suddenly gone; no pratfall or smile can get him out of this one. The machine gun fires several times and he is simply gone. As many times as I have seen this film, his death still affects me deeply. The film ends with the narrator talking about the gift that his father gave to him.

Key Sequence: 1:35:20–1:38:49

No scene better captures the conflicting tone of the film than this one, where Guido plays the music for Dora, his "Princess." As the song plays, the camera seems to become one with the sound waves carrying the tune, drifting out the window, over barbed-wire fences to reach Dora, who moves toward the window to hear. The director crosscuts between Dora and Guido, using close-ups and positioning them in the frame so they look like they could be facing each other. On his way back to the barracks, Guido is carrying Joshua through the heavy fog we saw at the beginning and wondering what they will do when they wake up from this dream. As he rounds a corner, lost, he stumbles onto a huge mound of human bones and ash: the magical faces reality. This is the horror that the narrator, who, as we learn later, is Joshua, has been protected from by his father.

Discussion Questions

1. Even though Guido and Dora never see each other while in the camp, how does he try to maintain their connection? How does the director maintain that connection for the audience? Why is this connection important to us?

2. Why do you think the director chose to have Guido die at the end of the film? How would it be different if he did not die?

How does the director film Guido's death? Why is this scene so powerful?

3. What, then, is the meaning of the title? What is the gift that the narrator (Joshua) says that his father gave him? How is this film a fable, like he said it was at the beginning?

Closing Questions/Activities

1. Choose a scene from this film and a similar scene from *Schindler's List* or another Holocaust film. What is similar and different between them? Why is this? What is different about the purposes of the two films?

2. Write a letter from an adult Joshua's point of view to his dead father thanking him for what he did.

3. How does this film fit into the fable genre? What are the magical moments, and what are the realistic moments? What lesson or moral does it teach us?

4. Write a letter to the editor about how this film trivializes the atrocities of the Holocaust, or write a letter defending its sometimes-humorous portrayal.

Frankenstein and *Bride of Frankenstein*

1931 and 1935, Not Rated, Directed by James Whale

Rationale

I guarantee that when you ask your students if they have heard of Frankenstein, all hands will go up, but if you ask whether they have seen either of these original Frankenstein films, you will be lucky if one says yes. From the moment that Boris Karloff put on the makeup in 1931, Frankenstein's monster never left our popular culture: spoofs and remakes seem to happen every few years. The story of Dr. Frankenstein and his creation (the kids always think that the monster is named "Frankenstein") is really one of our best modern myths, and the issues it raises about playing God and about the role of science are probably more relevant in our postnuclear, genetics-altering society today than they were in the 1930s when these films were made. The day I write this, a team of scientists is announcing that it has created Andi, a rhesus monkey with jellyfish DNA. The two films are also wonderful examples of the effect of German Expressionism in cinema, and they rank among the best horror movies ever made, though your students most likely have a different conception of the horror genre. Taken separately, each film tells only part of the story, but if you were to teach both (they are very short films), your students would see the full cycle of the story that Mary Shelley subtitled *A Modern Prometheus*. Each film is broken into two Viewing Days, though you may want to have a class day in between to discuss issues raised by the first film before moving on. These two are the oldest of all the films in this book, and they certainly are dated in terms of set, sound, costume, and make-up. There are also moments of writing that fall a bit flat and chance coincidences at which students may groan or laugh, but, overall, students seem to appreciate the chance to see something that they thought they knew a lot about but probably would not have seen on their own.

Previewing

1. Popular culture images: Ask students what they know about the Frankenstein story, focusing especially on the monster and what he looks like or acts like. Have your students draw pictures of what they imagine the monster to look like. If you have Internet capabilities at your school, you might take a look at an interesting Web site featuring artwork, submitted by people around the world, that was inspired by the novel and the films. The site, which has been in place for a number of years, keeps a gallery of the work that your students can look at and compare with their own. You can find the site at: http://www.cityu.edu.hk/ls/research/frankenstein/item1.htm

2. Theme: Ask students to share their feelings about science. Should scientists . . .

   ▪ be allowed to alter the genes of an unborn child to increase intelligence or strength, or change hair color or gender?

   ▪ experiment on prisoners or mentally disabled persons if the work will benefit humanity? (Note: Be aware that this question can generate much debate. I have found that more students than you might imagine answer yes.)

   ▪ genetically alter animals or crops to better feed humans?

   ▪ conduct experiments that may lead to the discovery of more powerful weapons?

   You may think of other questions that could lead students to examine the ethical boundaries of science.

3. Genre: Most students know the horror genre today only in terms of the "slasher" films that have come back into vogue with the *Scream* series. However, these films employ many conventions that first appeared in *Frankenstein* and similar monster/gothic films. Ask students to make lists of horror films they have seen and to describe how they know that they are watching a horror film as soon as it comes on TV. They

will mention such things as lighting, mood, shocking surprises, violence, and so on.

4. German Expressionism: To help your students appreciate these films, I suggest that you spend a bit of time talking about the German Expressionist movement in art, since so much of it found its way into Hollywood filmmaking. From the beginning of the twentieth century through the 1920s, artists such as Edvard Munch, Ernst Ludwig Kirchner, and Wassily Kandinsky were creating artwork that celebrated the hallucinatory images of dreams and nightmares. Disorder and doom echoed through their paintings of subjects caught in upheaval and madness. Many students are familiar with Munch's painting *The Scream*, an early example of this style, in which a tortured man's screams ripple around him in color and texture. In film, *The Cabinet of Dr. Caligari* is a famous—and readily available for rental or purchase—example of Expressionism: the sets' lines are often slanted, the angles are awkward, and the lighting creates pockets of shadows throughout the scenes. Other famous examples are *M*, starring Peter Lorre, and many American film noirs, such as *Night of the Hunter* and *Double Indemnity*, both of which came after *Frankenstein*.

Frankenstein

Viewing Day #1: 0:00:00–0:34:06 (about 34 minutes)

-   Begins with: opening credits
-   Ends with: the monster being put into the dungeon

Things to Notice

The mood is set immediately with the low-key lighting in the graveyard surrounded by the starkly barren landscape. As Frankenstein and Fritz (what, no Igor?) dig, they even throw dirt onto the statue of the grim reaper, as if to show Frankenstein's scorn for death. Frankenstein's laboratory sits high upon a cliff, impossibly gothic. This scenery contrasts sharply with the "real world" of Elizabeth and Henry's father, where order and light dominate even the *very* bad acting. The scene where the monster comes to life remains very effective even by today's standards (see Key Sequence below), and, the first time we see the monster alive, the director cuts very quickly with low-angle shots that give us a distorted sense of the monster at first. When the monster is locked in the dungeon, notice the twisted lines of the backdrop and the shadowy, low-key light: it is something right out of *Dr. Caligari*.

Key Sequence: 0:22:00–0:25:36

It has to be the "It's Alive! It's Alive!" scene, right? It's one of the most famous scenes in film history. The quick cuts, the expressionistic lighting, and the truly deranged performance of Colin Clive make this sequence the nightmarish climax of the film's first half.

Discussion Questions

1. What motivates Henry Frankenstein to do what he does? Why are some people repulsed by what he does?

2. What are your feelings about the monster at this point? Based only on what you have seen so far, is he evil? What does Frankenstein himself think of his creation? Why does he call the monster "it" and not "him"?

3. Why do you think Elizabeth is in this movie? What is her role, and what is her effect on Frankenstein?

Viewing Day #2: 0:35:06–1:11:00 (about 36 minutes)

- Begins with: the monster escaping for the first time (he escapes often)
- Ends with: closing credits

Things to Notice

When Frankenstein is back home with Elizabeth, thinking that the monster will be killed by his colleague, the set lines, lighting, and costumes all signal a return to normalcy (birds are even chirping in the background!), and, in fact, Frankenstein tells her that he wants to forget about that "nightmare." The nightmare, however, is going to intrude on his waking life because his doctor friend forgot to tie the monster down. Remember, the stupidity of the characters is a common element of all horror films. The scene with the monster and the little girl also ranks high on famous-shot lists and hints at the humanity of the monster and his desire for contact and communication (see Figure 33). Be sure that you have the original version, which shows the monster actually throwing the little girl into the water—some later versions omitted it. When you see the original version, you understand that the monster kills the girl out of misunderstanding, not viciousness. With the monster on the loose, Frankenstein's home begins to take on some of the same mazelike qualities of his laboratory castle. The crowd soon pursues the monster to the same barren landscape of the opening, and, after Frankenstein confronts his creation (see Figure 34), the monster is burned, and things are returned to normal, with Henry taken safely back home.

Figure 33. Probably the most tender moment in *Frankenstein*, and one of the few brightly lit outdoor scenes. Unfortunately, the monster's attempt at communication goes badly awry.

Figure 34. "Father" and "son" in *Frankenstein:* Notice the expressionistic lighting, the high angle, and the faceless crowd below.

Key Sequence: 1:00:00–1:04:00

What do you say to your son who has been behaving badly? What would you say to a father who has abandoned you? The monster cannot speak until the second film, and there are no words of apology from Frankenstein, who is bent solely on destroying him. There are a couple of nice shots when they look at each other through the spinning wheel, sizing each other up, and the framing seems to hint at an equality or at least a duality of the two men. As his punishment for pursuing power beyond his control, Henry is thrown from the mill like a rag doll (of course, it might have *been* a rag doll, with special effects being what they were). The screams of the monster as he burns in the fire are pitiful and affecting. But we do get a type of happy ending when Frankenstein is returned to his house and nursed by Elizabeth.

Discussion Questions

1. What are your feelings about the monster now? Is he human, an evil monster, a lost soul? What does he appear to want? Do you have sympathy for him?

2. How do you feel about Frankenstein? Was he punished for his actions? Do you feel sympathy for him?

3. How are the townspeople portrayed? Why do you think this is?

4. This film was made in 1931. What aspects of the film seem very dated to you, and what elements still seem powerful?

Bride of Frankenstein

Viewing Day #3: 0:00:00–0:35:45 (about 36 minutes)

- Begins with: opening credits
- Ends with: the monster hearing the blind man play

Things to Notice

The "frame" of the story starts with Lord Byron, Percy Bysshe Shelley, and Mary Wollstonecraft Shelley on the famous night where she reportedly came up with the idea of the monster. Be sure to notice that the actress who plays Mary Shelley—Elsa Lanchester—also plays the intended bride of the monster. We learn very quickly that the monster is not dead, and he immediately and rather brutally dispatches two people, as an owl looks on indifferently. Frankenstein's home in this one is very gothic in form, and when the evil Dr. Pretorius arrives on urgent and "grave" business (his bad pun not mine), the lighting causes ripples like firelight behind him and the eerie music suggests his evil plan to draw Frankenstein back to the dark side. The laboratory of Dr. Pretorius is very expressionistic in lighting and angular set design, and, though Frankenstein is appalled, he is tempted to continue his work. In marked contrast, the next time that we see the monster, he is in a lush, naturalistic setting with magical, romantic music playing in the background (see Key Sequence below). When he is captured, he is bound to a stake and held upright, not accidentally looking like Christ on a crucifix. This idea of the monster as a persecuted figure is reinforced by the soft, sacred-sounding organ music as the monster approaches the blind man.

Key Sequence: 0:25:13–0:27:05

In this idyllic setting, the monster sees his own reflection and is horrified at his own nature. This is the first in a series of moments that are part of his growing self-awareness. When he sees the beautiful shepherdess, he seeks contact and communication, and, when she falls, he clearly has learned from his first disaster with water, so he tries to save her. Once again, though, he kills without knowing why.

Discussion Questions

1. How does Frankenstein feel about what he did in the first film? How has he suffered for it already?

2. How is Frankenstein different from Dr. Pretorius? Why are we somewhat sympathetic to Frankenstein but not to Pretorius?

3. Think back on the music, framing, and lighting choices that the director has used for the monster so far in this film. What was he hoping to achieve? How is this approach different from that of the first film?

4. Much was made in the first film of the monster having the abnormal brain of a criminal, but little has been said of it in this one. Why do you think this is?

Viewing Day #4: 0:35:45–1:13:36 (about 38 minutes)

- Begins with: the monster going into the hermit's home
- Ends with: closing credits

Things to Notice

The monster is finally successful at doing what he had been trying to do—apparently—over the course of two films: to communicate with another human being. These scenes with the blind hermit are the most tender shots in both films, and the monster learns the word "friend." When he is chased out, however, he goes back to a graveyard because he was told that he came from dead bodies: the monster appears to have a growing sense of himself, which hints at his suicide at the end. Another Christlike image appears as the monster descends into the mausoleum. Frankenstein, too, has occasions when he knows himself: he seems to know that a woman was killed to get the heart he needs in order to build the monster bride that will get his Elizabeth back (she has been kidnapped by Dr. Pretorius), though his guilt—as always—passes quickly. As the two doctors work on creating the bride, the director gives us a series of Dutch angles, quick cuts, and sharp, direct lighting to demonstrate the madness of their actions. And, once again, Colin Clive gets to utter (a variation of) the line that he does so well: "She's alive!"

Key Sequence: 0:36:45–0:40:07

As the monster enters the hermit's home, he is treated gently for the first time in his existence, and the soft organ music signifies that maybe the hermit is right in thinking that the monster is a gift from God. After eating, the monster weeps along with the hermit, and a glowing crucifix can be seen just over the monster's shoulder.

Discussion Questions

1. How does Frankenstein feel about seeing his creation again? How does the director convey this feeling to us?
2. Why is Frankenstein not sickened by his female creation? What causes her reaction to the monster?
3. Why does the monster commit suicide? Why does he kill Pretorius but allow Frankenstein to leave?
4. Why all the Christ images in this second film? What is the director trying to say about Frankenstein the monster, and about the crowd's treatment of him?

Discussion Questions That Cannot Be Answered

1. Why is there always a thunderstorm at exactly the right moment for the creating of life?
2. How does Elizabeth escape?
3. Why does the most annoying character, Minnie the housekeeper, not die?

Closing Questions/Activities

1. The monster appears to become whatever people expect him to be. Explain his behavior by looking at his interactions throughout the films with the little girl, the townspeople, the hermit, and Drs. Pretorius and Frankenstein.

2. In the novel, the monster kills Elizabeth, so Frankenstein must suffer for trying to play God. In both films, however, Frankenstein and Elizabeth escape without serious harm. In what ways does the director criticize Frankenstein's actions? Is society to blame somehow? Look at how everyone treats Frankenstein.

3. Look at one of the remakes or spoofs of the Frankenstein story. What elements are the same in the remakes and what has been changed? What are the effects of the changes?

4. The image that we have of the monster in our popular culture is that of Boris Karloff's squared head and bolted neck, but that is not the description of the monster in Mary Shelley's novel. Read or skim through passages of the novel to find out how the creature is described. Draw pictures of what Shelley imagined the creature to be and compare it with the images in the film.

5. Watch the film *Gods and Monsters,* which recounts the final days of the director of both of these Frankenstein films, James Whale. Watch for scenes from the films and examine their role in this newer film. What did the monster mean to Whale? (Teachers: Note that this film is rated R.)

Rocky

1976, Rated PG, Directed by John G. Avildsen

Rationale

I fully admit that this one might be a tough sell at first glance, but as Robin Knapp, a teacher from Fulton County, Georgia, told me when she suggested its worthiness, "What is more American than a rags-to-riches underdog story?" The Rocky movies have been widely attacked, mostly justifiably, but that really has nothing to do with the first Rocky film, which, when you look back at it, is a tender, careful, accurate, and only slightly sentimentalized portrait of the American Dream—which, by the way, won an Academy Award for Best Picture. So, for an eleventh-grade class, studying American literature, *Rocky* fits in well with the mythological promises of this country. I have found, too, that under direct questioning, very few students have actually seen the first Rocky film. The music, the dialogue, the mise-en-scène of working-class Philadelphia, and the rapid editing of the final fight sequence make this film quite worthwhile for both thematic and cinematic study. The film also helped popularize the whole genre of sports films. Now, if *Rocky* is out of stock at the video store and you're thinking about substituting *Rocky IV* or *Rocky V*, don't do it!

Previewing

1. Theme: I would suggest starting with the mythology of the American Dream, and what it is that the United States appears to promise anyone, regardless of divisions such as social class, gender, and ethnicity. Why is this mythology important to Americans? What real-life examples of the dream can you name? What classifies someone as an underdog? Why do Americans tend to root for the underdog? Who are our American heroes today? What do we look for in our heroes?

2. Plot: Which of the five (as I write this, there are rumors of another!) Rocky films have you seen? What do they all have in common? How are they different? Why do you think that critics have not cared for the later films?

3. Setting: The American bicentennial in 1976 was a celebratory time of patriotism. Why do you think this time period, and the setting of Philadelphia, were chosen?

Viewing Day #1: 0:00:00–0:28:44 (about 29 minutes)

- Begins with: familiar-sounding, Rocky-theme trumpet music
- Ends with: Rocky walking the teenage girl home

Things to Notice

The very first image we see in the film after the word "Rocky" rolls across the screen is of Jesus Christ looking down on a darkened boxing hall. Two fighters—we know one is Rocky, surely—fight in front of a sign that reads "Resurrection" and a crowd that is bored and angry. The fight turns dirty, and Rocky wins by beating his opponent brutally; afterward, the two receive their tiny payouts while Rocky smokes. The remainder of this day's viewing establishes the film's setting and Rocky's character. There is a wonderful scene of him returning from the fight to his apartment (see Key Sequence below). We learn that he works part-time for a loan shark, but that he "ain't emotionally involved" in it. We see that he is a rescuer of people and lost things: he takes a drunk man inside from the street and tries to lecture a young girl about hanging out on the street. But throughout today's viewing are hints that things are not going well: his locker is taken from him at the boxing ring; he visits a woman (Adrian) at the pet store, but they are separated by images of mirrors and cages; Paulie tells him, "Start living your life or your body starts to dry up"; and the bartender talks about the need to take a shot in life.

Key Sequence: 0:06:56–0:09:41

After Rocky returns to his apartment from the first fight, we see a poster of his namesake, Rocky Marciano, hanging over his mantel. In front of a mirror (there are many mirrors in this film for the characters' times of self-reflection), we see a picture of a young boy, and, as the camera moves in closer, there is only the picture and Rocky's reflection in the frame. Rocky looks back and forth between the picture and his image, as if trying to find a resemblance. His bed is a single, and hanging above it is a crucifix.

Discussion Questions

1. What do we learn about Rocky from his actions and from the mise-en-scène in this section? How does Sylvester Stallone's performance contribute to how we feel about him?

2. What does the director do to help create the mood and tone of this film through lighting and music?

3. The words "loser" and "bum" have already come up and will continue to be heard throughout the film. Why are those words so emotionally charged? How does Rocky react to them?

4. Notice how often Rocky is framed alone in a long shot. What is the effect?

Viewing Day #2: 0:28:30–0:53:14 (about 25 minutes)

- Begins with: Apollo and his promoters
- Ends with: Adrian and Rocky kissing

Things to Notice

When Apollo's promoter says it's very American to give a nobody a title shot, Apollo corrects him by saying, no, it's very smart, which shows the cynicism that some characters have toward the American Dream and toward Rocky. The teenage girl that Rocky tried to help is back out on the corner. When Rocky and Adrian go skating on their date, there is a growing connection: Rocky says his father told him that he had no brains, so he'd better develop his body, while Adrian's mother told her that she had no body, so she'd better develop her brain. Opposites attract? Rocky tells her he started fighting to prove that he's not a bum. Adrian makes a decision to go inside Rocky's apartment, where they kiss. The theme of taking a shot and trying to love ripples throughout the film.

Key Sequence: 0:46:02–0:53:14

Outside of Rocky's apartment, Adrian hesitates, unsure of herself and of Rocky. Inside, their costume choices—Rocky in a T-shirt and Adrian in her hat and coat—contrast with each other, and Adrian is framed in a long shot to emphasize their distance. The framing changes to close-ups, however, once they grow more intimate. The diegetic song's chorus is, "I'll take you away."

Discussion Questions

1. How is Adrian's character revealed through costume choices and the performance of Talia Shire? How is she similar to and different from Rocky?

2. Part of the theme of this film is that in order to live you've got to take your shot at life. What difficult choice did Adrian make? What holds her back? Why did she do it?

3. Eventually we know that Rocky Balboa will fight Apollo Creed. What images do their names conjure up? How are the names in conflict with each other?

4. In what ways do Apollo and the promoters appear to be cynical about the American Dream and its promises?

Viewing Day #3: 0:53:14–1:25:12 (about 32 minutes)

- Begins with: Rocky going into boxing gym
- Ends with: Apollo's trainer watching Rocky hit the meat

Things to Notice

Mick, who runs the boxing ring, tells Rocky that he is washed up just when Rocky gets a message to meet with the promoter of the Apollo Creed fight. The promoter talks about America as the land of opportunity, and the camera moves in on Rocky as he makes his choice to fight, to take his shot. At the ensuing press conference with Apollo, Rocky is made to look foolish on TV (see Figure 35). A pitiful Mick comes to see Rocky to let him train him for the fight. He brings along his aged press clippings from his prime, but Rocky cuts him off by saying, "At least

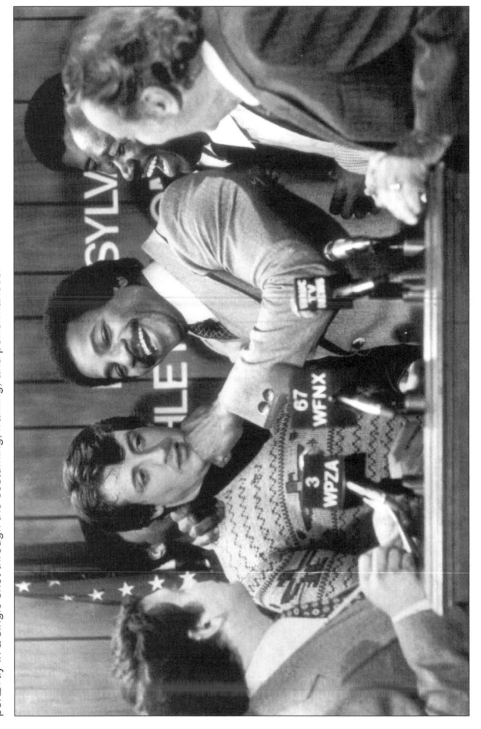

Figure 35. He's the butt of everyone's joke in *Rocky*. The movie's theme of overcoming low expectations is captured perfectly in a single shot through the costuming, framing, and performances.

you had a prime." Because of Rocky's giving nature, however, he relents, though the reconciliation is seen in a long shot and not played for sentimentality. Rocky then begins his first training day (see Key Sequence below), and the day's viewing ends with the contrasting images of Rocky beating up the hanging meat and Apollo discussing finances and box office receipts.

Key Sequence: 1:10:16–1:13:48

The first morning of training begins at 4 A.M. It is cold and lonely-seeming, and Rocky is moving slowly and awkwardly. His outfit is old and the music is stripped down—just a bare horn and piano. The scene, like so many in the film, has Rocky alone and framed in a long shot, which emphasizes that he is both a part of his surroundings and isolated from them. After he struggles to make it up to the top of the steps, we see him in a high angle with the cityscape in the distance.

Discussion Questions

1. How do we know that Rocky was affected by what happened at the press conference? What clues do we have that most people seem to underestimate Rocky?
2. Why is the fight with Mick in Rocky's apartment so emotional? What is each character bringing to that argument? How does the director add to the emotion of the scene through framing and editing?
3. Why is that first training morning so important? What do we learn about Rocky? How would you describe the mood or tone of that scene? What contributed to the mood and tone?

Viewing Day #4: 1:25:12–end (about 32 minutes)

- Begins with: Paulie coming home with a wreath
- Ends with: closing credits

Things to Notice

Paulie has difficulties with Rocky and Adrian, and they all have a fight while the diegetic music "Silent Night" plays in the background. We then see the famous Rocky training montage, set to the nondiegetic "Gonna Fly Now." This time we see him in close and medium shots along with other people, and the sequence ends with his quick assent to the top of the art museum steps in sharp contrast to his earlier training scene. If you remember this film as being a boxing movie, it's odd that the big fight starts with only ten minutes remaining in the film. The fight sequence is a textbook study of the use of close-ups, pacing, sound effects, music, overhead shots, and reaction shots. Even twenty years later, it is highly effective and moving; everything has a particular purpose and effect. The fifteenth and final round is seen in its entirety, and, when it ends, there is a mass of confusion (see Key Sequence below), but it doesn't matter—Rocky went the distance and thus has triumphed.

Key Sequence: 1:55:05–end

The final scene deserves to be reexamined because it is so unusual not to have the dramatic arm-raising as the winner is announced. After the final bell rings, the music swells and soars, and the director gives us a series of quick cuts, swish pans, and overlapping dialogue that perhaps tries to establish what Rocky's mind might be like at this moment. Reporters are hurling questions at him, but he's shouting for Adrian, and the announcer is saying that Apollo won on a split decision, though no one but Apollo appears to care. The film ends not with the victory of a prizefight, but with a slow-motion close-up of Rocky and Adrian saying that they love each other.

Discussion Questions

1. Why was Paulie so upset with Rocky and Adrian? What did they get that he did not? How does Rocky try to help him?

2. What makes the training sequence so effective? How do the pacing, music, and performances contribute to the feelings you get from watching it? How does this sequence contrast with the depiction of Rocky's previous training?

3. Why is the ending shot like it is? Why do we not see a dramatic raising of the winner's arm like in most real and fictional boxing matches?

Closing Questions/Activities

1. Is Rocky an American hero? Why or why not? What attributes make him a hero? What are we supposed to feel about him, and what causes us to feel that way?

2. One theme that runs through this film is the value of taking a chance. How is this theme dramatized in the movie? Who takes chances, who doesn't, and what are the results?

3. Look at the other Rocky films. What do they do that is different from or similar to this one? Why have they been less critically successful?

4. Research Sylvester Stallone's work to get *Rocky* made. How do his own experiences parallel or diverge from Rocky's?

Smoke Signals

1998, Rated PG-13, Directed by Chris Eyre

Rationale

If you ever want to bet on which groups have been most unfairly represented by Hollywood, I would not advise betting against American Indians. For fifty or more years, they were portrayed as evil savages bent on keeping White America from fulfilling its Manifest Destiny. When Hollywood became more historically sensitive, American Indians, with some exceptions, became stock mystical characters used by White characters to work out their own identity issues (e.g., *Dances with Wolves* and *Little Big Man*). But *Smoke Signals* is a film written by, directed by, and starring American Indians, and the result is a funny and emotionally powerful portrayal of contemporary American Indian life. The film was written by Sherman Alexie, who adapted several of his own short stories, and it revolves around two teenagers—Thomas and Victor—as they leave their reservation for the first time. The movie is at times the visual equivalent of the oral tradition of American Indian storytelling, as it seamlessly shifts its time period, location, and tone. If the ending is a bit too neat, the filmmakers should be forgiven when one considers everything else they try—and succeed in doing.

Previewing

1. Representation in film: I start teaching this film by asking students to list films or TV shows in which American Indians play a part. (One class needed some prompting, so I brought in a few Westerns to help them get going. John Wayne films in particular work well because of references made by characters in *Smoke Signals*.) I then ask students to describe how American Indians tend to be represented.

2. Theme: One of the most important themes in this film is that we need to listen to other people's stories so that we can truly understand them. Ask students to describe stories that their parents, grandparents, or older siblings have told them about things that happened before they were born. Why do people tell stories? Why is it important to listen to them?

3. Plot: This film is about a journey and the discovery that comes along the way. Why are journeys important, and what kinds of things can we learn from them? Why do we sometimes come to understand things only when we are away from them?

Viewing Day #1: 0:00:00–0:29:48 (about 30 minutes)

- Begins with: Opening credits
- Ends with: Thomas telling his story about Denny's

Things to Notice

The film opens up almost immediately with a fire—the writer and director intended to include the four classic elements (fire, earth, air, and water)—in their story. Much of this day's viewing is spent in going back and forth in time to establish the difficult relationship between Victor and Thomas (see Key Sequence below) and in giving the audience a sense of reservation life. It becomes clear that Thomas is a storyteller and is partial to funny, poignant anecdotes, though we are not always sure if his stories are true. We also know that Victor does not care for Thomas's stories at all, probably because Victor's own stories seem to be about only pain and loss.

Key Sequence: 0:09:00–0:15:47

This is a wonderful series of scenes to reexamine for editing. It starts when Victor is in the store and Thomas first asks to go with him. We then see a smooth flashback of Victor and his father and return to the present. Then we crosscut between the two boys' homes and the women who take care of them. The parallels and connections are made through gestures, actions, and framing choices. The segment ends when Victor tells Thomas that he can go.

Discussion Questions

1. What is the effect of all of the time shifts in the film? Do we ever feel lost or confused? What does the director do to help us follow?

2. Describe the life depicted on the reservation so far. What do you think are the writer's and/or director's feelings about the reservation?

3. How are Victor and Thomas different? How are they similar? What do they each think of Victor's father?

Viewing Day #2: 0:29:48–1:00:36 (about 31 minutes)

- Begin with: Victor's painful flashback about his father's leaving
- Ends with: Victor going into his father's trailer

Things to Notice

Victor tries to teach Thomas how to "be a real Indian," though after the lesson the boys are insulted by two cowboys who have stolen their seats on the bus. The reality of life off the reservation is made clear for them. When Thomas asks Suzy, who contacted Victor about his father's death, to tell a story, she asks, "Do you want the truth or lies?" and Thomas replies, "I want both." She does tell a story about meeting Victor's father, Arnold, and she narrates a story that Arnold told her about a time when he and Victor beat some Jesuits at basketball (see Key Sequence below). Victor corrects her and tells her that they lost that game. Suzy is an odd character: we do not know enough about her to understand her motivations and emotions, though the filmmakers probably did this on purpose—perhaps they intended for her to remain a mysterious character, capable of understanding both the material and the mystical worlds.

Key Sequence: 0:51:54–0:54:28

This is the scene where Suzy tells Victor about Arnold's story of playing basketball against the priests: it is a flashback within a flashback, with quick takes, dramatic music, and lighting. Arnold has never been so confident and alive in the entire film.

Discussion Questions

1. Everyone in the film seems to like to tell and hear stories except Victor. Why do you think this is? Are the stories that Thomas tells the truth or fiction? Does it matter?

2. What does Victor think of as a "real Indian"? Why do they sing "John Wayne's Teeth"? Why does the song switch from diegetic to nondiegetic, and how is it different when it becomes nondiegetic?

3. Describe Suzy's character. What purpose is she serving in the story? What is she trying to teach Victor?

Viewing Day #3: 1:00:36–1:23:00 (about 23 minutes)

- Begins with: Victor in his father's trailer
- Ends with: closing credits

Things to Notice

When Victor is in his father's trailer, he sees a picture of himself, his mother, and his father with the word "Home" written on the back. He then cuts off his hair in a ceremony similar to what Arnold did after the fire years ago. On the way back home in Arnold's truck, Thomas tells Victor that "we're traveling heavy with illusion," and they get into a fight about Victor's behavior since Arnold left him. The two come across a car accident, and, as Victor runs to try to get help, he has visions of his father, but this time they are from the stories that Thomas and Suzy gave him, not necessarily the images of his own painful past: he has begun listening to stories. They drive back to the reservation to the nondiegetic music "Father and Farther" (see Key Sequence below). The film ends with the camera moving across a raging river to see Victor scattering his father's ashes from the bridge that Thomas told him about. His shouts blend into those of a traditional-sounding chant as the camera sweeps over his head and returns to the water, in perfect contrast to the fire of the opening. We then hear Thomas wondering, "If we forgive our fathers, what is left?"

Key Sequence: 1:13:56–1:16:00

As Thomas and Victor drive away after meeting with the police, we hear the song "Father and Farther." The camera goes high overhead and seems to beat them home to capture scenes of the reservation. Meanwhile we crosscut to Suzy burning down Arnold's trailer. Arnold's grief may have started in that fire years ago, but now he can be cleansed by fire once the truth is revealed.

Discussion Questions

1. Listen again to the lyrics of "Father and Farther." Even though this song was not written specifically for the film, it fits very well. How does it relate to and comment on the events that have been depicted?

2. What is Suzy's role in this film? Think about her statement that she kept Arnold's secrets, her attempt to help Victor forgive, and the fact that she burns the trailer down.

3. What do you make of the film's ending? How have things changed for Victor? Is anything different for Thomas?

Closing Questions/Activities

1. In Hebrew the name "Thomas" means "good company," and in Latin "Victor" means "conquering." How did these two characters play out their own names in this film?

2. The writer originally wanted to have all the basketball scenes played outdoors like the one where Arnold talks to Suzy, but it rained on the days they were supposed to film. Why do you

think he wanted the scenes outdoors, and how would that have compared with what is in fact on the screen? Explain.

3. A line of dialogue that was cut from the very end of the film has Thomas asking Victor if he might listen to one of his stories sometime, and Victor says yes. What role do stories and the art of storytelling play in this film? Why are stories important?

4. Read one or more of the stories from the collection *The Lone Ranger and Tonto Fistfight in Heaven* by Sherman Alexie, the screenwriter of the film (the story "This Is What It Means to Say Phoenix, Arizona" is the one related most directly to the film). What elements of his stories about reservation life are similar to or different from the film? How have the characters—Thomas in particular—been changed?

Cyrano de Bergerac

1990, Rated PG, Directed by Jean-Paul Rappeneau

Rationale

The 1950s version with Jose Ferrer is very good, but this updated version in French—with artfully constructed subtitles by Anthony Burgess—is a beautiful film that takes students beyond the image of Cyrano as a swashbuckling, big-nosed loser to the image of a true Romantic individualist. This is a long and complex film, but a rewarding one with impressive costumes and sets, as well as an amazing performance by Gerard Depardieu as Cyrano.

Previewing

1. Reading subtitles: If your students have not watched a foreign-language film—and most will not do so voluntarily—you will probably want to have them practice reading subtitles. See the discussion of *Life is Beautiful* for a description of an activity that I find helpful.

2. Character (part one): Many students already know the idea of Cyrano as the man who helped another man persuade a woman to fall in love with him. As a way of getting students to see this and other sides of his character, I recommend showing students clips from the Steve Martin movie *Roxanne,* which is an adaptation of the Cyrano story. I have shown my students the opening sequence where "C. D." (Martin) duels two obnoxious drunk men with his tennis racket, the scene in the bar where he comes up with his own creative insults about his large nose, and the scene where he takes over for Chris

beneath Roxanne's balcony. I then ask students to make a list of C. D.'s characteristics. If a class is having difficulty with *Cyrano de Bergerac*, I will show key scenes from *Roxanne* between viewing days of *Cyrano*, to help students follow the main action.

3. Character (part two): Cyrano is a Romantic—note the capital "R"—and not necessarily just because he is interested in romance (which is what students automatically tend to assume). I think it's important that students understand the ideas of the Romantic philosophy: the emphasis of emotion over reason, the image of the individual unbound by unnecessary traditions, and the quest for truth and beauty in all things.

Viewing Day #1: 0:00:00–0:29:07 (about 29 minutes)

- Begins with: opening credits
- Ends with: Cyrano's fight with the soldiers

Things to Notice

This film of a play starts with a play, and a running theme throughout is that Cyrano sees himself as a supporting player in a play of his life. We see the wonders of the playhouse through the eye-line matches of a child's view. When we see Roxane during this first part, she is bathed in light and shot in soft focus, often from the point of view of Christian, who is in love with her. It is interesting that we hear Cyrano before we see him, and, whenever we do see him in these opening scenes, he is bold, strong, confident, and quick to find and defend against insults, whether perceived or real. Through some early eye-line matches, we get hints that he too is fond of Roxane. At the very end of the day's viewing, the director chooses to show Cyrano battling the hired soldiers through the fog and in slow motion, pointing to his almost superhuman abilities.

Key Sequence: 0:15:00–0:17:20

While maybe not so interesting cinematically, this is a great scene to rewatch just to give students the chance to understand the language and appreciate Depardieu's performance. This is when Cyrano comes up with his own insults for his large nose. There are some wonderful puns and other jokes that probably cannot be caught on the first viewing.

Discussion Questions

1. What do you find interesting, new, or confusing about the movie so far? Are you able to follow the action and the sub-

titles at the same time? Did you ever feel yourself getting lost? If so, when?

2. How would you describe Cyrano's character? How has he demonstrated these qualities so far? How has the director helped us to feel this way about Cyrano?

Viewing Day #2: 0:29:07–0:55:51 (about 27 minutes)

- Begins with: the pastry cook writing his poetry
- Ends with: Roxane swooning after reading the letters

Things to Notice

When Cyrano and Roxane meet, there are close-ups, high-key lighting, and a natural scenery backdrop. You may want to point out how often Cyrano is framed alone in the shot. When de Guiche asks Cyrano if he's read *Don Quixote*, Cyrano replies, "I've practically lived it." The true optimism of Cyrano comes through when de Guiche tells him that the windmills that he chases will spin him down into the mud, but Cyrano suggests, "Or up to the stars."

Key Sequence: 0:45:07–0:47:25

Again, a wonderful scene for language and performance, this is during Cyrano's "no merci" speech. His friend Le Bret tries to suggest that Cyrano could use a protector, but, with the refrain of "no merci," Cyrano retorts hotly, emphasizing the loss of individuality while being in service, though at the end of his rant he sits alone, quietly meditating on the struggle he faces because of his choices in life.

Discussion Questions

1. In addition to providing comedic relief, what other purpose does the pastry chef Ragueneau serve in the film? Think about his dual "arts" and the sacrifices he makes for each.

2. The concept of yin and yang is that two halves complement each other to form a complete whole. How do Cyrano and Christian fit into this concept?

3. What do you know about *Don Quixote*, and why is Cyrano compared to him in this section?

Viewing Day #3: 0:55:51–1:24:27 (about 30 minutes)

- Begins with: Roxane receiving more letters
- Ends with: Christian and Cyrano leaving for war

Things to Notice

Shots of Roxane are seen in the mirror when she is being duplicitous
with de Guiche, just as, later, Cyrano is hidden in shadow when he de-
scribes to de Guiche his fictitious trip to the moon. The balcony scene
(see Key Sequence below) plays beautifully with light and music and
comes at just about the middle point of the film. The day ends with an
effective high-angle long shot of Roxane and Cyrano just as he leaves
for war.

Key Sequence: 1:08:40–1:15:50

Everything in this balcony scene is designed to create a mood of magic
and romantic possibilities; not only must Cyrano convince Roxane of
his/Christian's love, but also Depardieu and the director must convince
the audience that his love is powerful enough for him to make all the
sacrifices he later makes. On both counts, they are successful because
of the wonderful use of high-key lighting on Roxane, dressed all in
white, as Cyrano moves from shadow to light, sometimes revealing and
sometimes obscuring himself from her—and obscuring the truth. Christian is almost entirely hidden in the dark, since this scene really belongs
to Cyrano and Roxane: it is the closest they ever come to being together.
As Christian scales the balcony to receive the kiss that Cyrano has
earned, we see Cyrano alone in a long shot, leaving them behind.

Discussion Questions

1. What do we learn about Roxane's character from the way that
   she treats Christian when he cannot speak as Cyrano writes?
   Why does she not suspect what should have been obvious to
   her?
2. In this day's viewing we saw how the political issues (the war)
   intrude upon the personal issues (their wedding night). When
   else have we seen this occur and what might it reveal about
   character or theme?

Viewing Day #4: 1:24:27–1:53:11 (about 29 minutes)

- Begins with: cadets leaving town
- Ends with: Christian's death and the battle afterward

Things to Notice

The mood has shifted noticeably, with low-key lighting, somber tones,
high angles, drab costuming, and mournful music to show the results
of the disastrous siege. The only glimmer of brightness comes in the form

of a somewhat muted Roxane, looking paler and older than she did in the city. As Christian dies, Cyrano gives him the ultimate gift by telling him that she chose Christian over himself.

Key Sequence: 1:46:40–1:51:00

Roxane declares her total love for Christian because of the soul that he has poured out in the letters he has sent her, though of course the letters and the soul really belong to Cyrano. Notice the front lighting on the animated Roxane and the side lighting on Christian as he tries to hide from the truth that is being revealed to him. Notice that when Christian runs away to fight in the battle, we do not actually see his enemy—he is just swinging his sword wildly back and forth. Cyrano has his one chance to declare his true love for her cut short when Roxane sees Christian hurt.

Discussion Questions

1. Are Cyrano and Christian truly yin and yang? Can they exist without each other?
2. How are these scenes during the siege different from the earlier scenes in the city? What has changed in the costumes, lighting, and music?
3. Is Roxane a fool? Is she naïve? Is she somewhat complicit in the tragedy that happens?

Viewing Day #5: 1:53:11–2:14:00 (about 21 minutes)

- Begins with: the nuns at the abbey where Roxane stays
- Ends with: closing credits

Things to Notice

Roxane is of course dressed in black, still in mourning over Christian's death, and Cyrano, too, is dressed in black. When Cyrano finally arrives after his accident, the two are in a naturalistic setting, similar to the one in Viewing Day #2, when he nearly proclaimed his love. The scene continues to grow darker as Cyrano's death approaches, matched by the growing awareness on Roxane's face as he reads "Christian's" final letter. His death scene (see Key Sequence below) brings together all the elements of his life that made up his tragedy.

Key Sequence: 2:08:03–end

Cyrano says that his legacy will be that he was everything and nothing and that his life's work was to serve as a prompter for others. As he dies, he moves away from his friends, since he has consistently faced everything by himself. He compares himself to Galileo and Socrates, each of whom also fought against falsehood, cowardice, and prejudice. Death and final judgment take everything, he says, but they cannot take his "panache," and, as he says it, he nearly gets his first kiss from Roxane, but even that escapes him. The camera pulls away slowly and we see the group from high overhead.

Discussion Questions

1. Why do you think the original writer—Edmond Rostand— wanted fifteen or more years to pass between the time of Christian's death and this final scene of Cyrano's death? What had happened to each character in the interim?

2. After saying goodbye to his friends, Cyrano goes off to die by himself. Why is this appropriate for him? How does the director shoot his death? What lighting, angles, framing, and music are used? For what effect?

3. What does Cyrano mean by his final dying words? What is "panache," and how does it relate to his character?

Closing Questions/Activities

1. Make a coat of arms for Cyrano. What important items would be included and why? What would he never put onto his coat of arms? Why?

2. If Cyrano were alive today in the United States, what would he be doing for a living and why? What kinds of things would he protest?

3. Watch a scene from *Roxanne* that is similar to one in *Cyrano*. What aspects are the same? What aspects are different and why? In what way are the purposes the same and different?

4. Write a love letter from Christian to Roxane; then edit it as if you were Cyrano.

Elizabeth

1998, Rated R, Directed by Shekhar Kapur

Rationale

A beautifully filmed depiction of the political troubles of Elizabeth I as she tries to bring together a nation divided over religion, this film would be a perfect companion to the study of British literature, commonly taught in the twelfth grade. The history, while not completely accurate, comes alive for students. The cinematography, which was nominated for an Academy Award, could be a textbook in itself for film technique and effect. One word of caution: the film is rated R, probably for violence and for three scenes that include sexuality and brief nudity.

Previewing

This film will need some front-loading for sure, since it deals with historical names, places, and events of which our students have little knowledge.

1. Time period: England was in the middle of its Renaissance period but deeply conflicted over issues of religion. Henry VIII separated England from the Catholic Church in 1534 and created his own Protestant Church of England. Queen Mary, the daughter of Henry VIII, was a devout Catholic but died in 1558 before she could produce an heir, so the Protestant Elizabeth, also the daughter of Henry, but of his second wife, Anne Boleyn, took over the throne. The film begins in 1554 and includes a brief summary of the political and religious conflicts, as well as a scene of Protestants being burned at the stake by Mary's followers. I would suggest showing just the first scene and discussing the time period before starting the film.

2. Characters. There are a lot of characters in this film, and, while the writers do a good job of establishing relationships, high school students may have difficulty following all the players on the first viewing of the film. I suggest a two-column list of Elizabeth's supporters, her opponents, and those about whom we are unsure. Through the various viewing days, students should add, change, and update their lists. The following list might get them started for the first viewing day:

Supporters	Opponents	Unsure
Sir Robert	Norfolk	Spanish Ambassador
Sir William		

3. Theme: What difficulties might a young woman have in trying to govern a nation in Elizabeth's time? What would you expect that she might have to give up in order to be successful as Queen? How might someone's personality have to change in order to become a strong leader?

Viewing Day #1: 0:00:00–0:30:48 (about 31 minutes)

- Begins with: opening credits
- Ends with: Elizabeth's coronation

Things to Notice

Starting with the stunning high-angle shots of the Protestants being burned, we learn of Mary's troubled reign in a very low-key-lit sequence. In sharp contrast is Elizabeth, stunning in costume and light, far away from the politics of the throne, dancing with her waiting women and her lover Robert. Elizabeth is soon arrested and taken to the Tower, where she is interrogated with a cross of light behind her, and the scene is shot with dizzying camera movements. The contrasts between the light of Elizabeth and the darkness of Mary continue until Mary dies and Elizabeth is named queen (see Key Sequence below).

Key Sequence: 0:26:33–0:30:48

The scene starts with the bell tolling the Queen's death and cuts back to the high-key-lit home of Elizabeth. As she walks outside, a bright light floods the frame, washing out the whole image, signaling perhaps a new and brighter future. In a long shot, we see Elizabeth alone, dressed in white, and then she receives the ring in a close-up and we see another flash of white. At her coronation, the director starts us high overhead, and as she takes on the crown, the scepter, and the orb, she seems quite overwhelmed.

Discussion Questions

1. What was Elizabeth like before she became Queen? How did she behave with Robert and her girls? How does the director show the intimacy between Elizabeth and Robert with music, lighting, and costumes?

2. Why does Robert tell her, "Remember who you are"? What does this expression mean?

3. Think back on the scenes in the Tower. How were they lit? Why? What was the director trying to communicate to the audience during Elizabeth's interrogation? How did he accomplish this?

4. Walsingham says, "You lose your innocence; you lose your soul." What do you think this means? What might it have to do with the rest of the film?

Viewing Day #2: 0:30:48–0:58:30 (about 28 minutes)

- Begins with: Elizabeth learning the Crown is bankrupt
- Ends with: Elizabeth meeting with the clergy
- Note: Sexual scene (with very brief nudity) at 0:00:16

Things to Notice

Elizabeth dances a second dance with Robert, but this time in public without apparent care of the scandal she causes. It becomes clearer that her true threat is Norfolk, who is almost always seen in a low angle and dressed in dark clothes. After her forces are defeated by Mary of Guise, Elizabeth is dwarfed by the enormity of her position, as suggested by a portrait of her father hanging overhead. The day ends, however, in her first triumph when she convinces the clergy to accept her resolution of unification of the two churches (see Key Sequence below).

Key Sequence: 0:52:56–0:57:35

Elizabeth prepares to meet the bishops of the Church to try to convince them to support her in her quest to unify England's religions. For an analysis of this scene, look back at the section of Chapter 3 that deals with characterization.

Discussion Questions

1. Elizabeth dances again with Robert in this section. How does she behave with him now? Has there been any change? What is the music like, and how do the spectators react to Elizabeth and Robert?

2. How does the slaughter of Elizabeth's invading forces affect her? Describe what the director did in the scene with her father's portrait? How is she framed? What does she learn from Walsingham?

3. Sir William states that Elizabeth's body is now the property of the state. Why does he say this? Does Elizabeth agree with this?

Viewing Day #3: 0:58:30–1:32:00 (about 34 minutes)

- Begins with: arrival of the French Duke
- Ends with: Walsingham meeting with Mary of Guise
- Note: Sexual situation (no nudity) at 1:25:52

Things to Notice

A very dangerous and unsteady viewing day for Elizabeth's reign. Elizabeth's suitor, Anjou from France, appears and brings a nice bit of comedic relief with him, though she will eventually reject him. Elizabeth dances a third dance with Robert (see Key Sequence below). Out of favor now, Robert again meets with the Spanish Ambassador in low-key lighting, somewhat obscured from the camera's view. The assassin, in a long shot, coming out of the shadows like a demon, nearly kills Elizabeth. Many of the shots in today's viewing seem to come in or go out through windows and curtains. Things do not appear safe, secure, or private today. It also appears that Walsingham, who has been a loyal supporter, is plotting against Elizabeth with Mary of Guise.

Key Sequence: 1:18:15–1:20:40

Perhaps because she wants to show off, Elizabeth calls Robert out of the shadows where he had been hiding to dance with her again. But this is not like the other dances: the two appear awkward and out of step with each other. When he tries to remind her that she is still "his Elizabeth" and lift her into the air like he had before, she angrily replies, "I am no man's Elizabeth!" The camera moves in close to Robert, alone again, but with a cut away to the Spanish Ambassador in order to foreshadow Robert's treason.

Discussion Questions

1. What has changed between Robert and Elizabeth? How has the director shown this growing distance?
2. Every time that Robert meets with the Spanish Ambassador, they are shown in shadows and behind objects. What is the effect of this lighting and camera placement?
3. The assassin/priest is loose at court. How does the director shoot him? Why?
4. How would you describe Walsingham? What is the nature of the advice that he gives Elizabeth? How is his advice different from the advice given by Robert and William?

Viewing Day #4: 1:32:00–end (26 minutes)

- Begins with: Robert telling Elizabeth to marry the king of Spain
- Ends with: closing credits
- Note: Sexual scene (with brief nudity) at 1:44:08

Things to Notice

Today Elizabeth becomes "her father's daughter," as one of her threats, Mary of Guise, is found dead, apparently by the hand of Walsingham. Look for the upside-down angles of the assassin as he is tortured by Walsingham—very effective in showing a turn in the balance of power. Elizabeth soon gathers all the information needed about the plot against her and, much like Michael Corleone at the end of *The Godfather,* she orders the capture and death of her enemies, though sparing Robert. Safe from her enemies, Elizabeth looks at a statue of the Virgin Mary and, taking Walsingham's advice that people need something greater than themselves to believe in, she transforms herself into the "Virgin Queen," dedicating herself to England (see Key Sequence below).

Key Sequence: 1:52:23–1:58:00

Soon after Elizabeth wonders if she "must be made of stone" to be as ruthless a leader as she has become, the director cuts to a shot of the Virgin Mary's head and matches it nicely to Elizabeth's head as she has her hair cut off. As she is painted white, she flashes back to key moments that led her to this point, most notably her first dance with Robert. With another brilliant flash of white, she presents herself to her people as the "Virgin Queen." When she speaks to Sir William, it is in a voice so deep and hollow that it's barely recognizable as hers. Notice too that as she passes by Robert, she does not even seem to notice him.

Discussion Questions

1. Why does Robert say that he conspired with Spain? Why does Elizabeth leave Robert alive?

2. What were your feelings about Elizabeth while the capture and executions were going on? Was she involved even though she was not present?

3. What does Elizabeth turn herself into at the end of the film? Why does she do this? How did the director shoot her in this final sequence? Why did he include the flashbacks of scenes while she is transforming herself? How are her waiting women dressed at the ceremony? Why?

Closing Questions/Activities

1. Trace the transformation of Elizabeth by looking at the three dances with Robert and her solo walk down the aisle at the end. How did the director show her growing confidence, independence, isolation, and strength through lighting, angles, costuming, and music?

2. Research the real-life events that were depicted in the film. What changes in chronology were made and for what dramatic purpose? Choose a character in the film and research his or her life to see if the representations in the film are consistent with historical fact. Are some characters fictional? What purpose(s) do they serve in the film?

3. Write a series of diary entries from Elizabeth's point of view at several key points in her life. Be sure that you include entries made both before she was Queen and during her troubled early reign, as well as a final entry about her decision to not marry. Include drawings or poems as well; the real Queen Elizabeth was a noted poet.

4. Two of the many themes in this film are the role of privacy in the public arena and the intrusion of the personal into the political world. How were these themes played out in cinematic, theatrical, and literary elements? How do such themes play out with political leaders in our own time?

Appendix A: Glossary of Film Terminology

Framing/Shots

- Long shot (LS): a shot taken from some distance; shows the full subject and perhaps the surrounding scene as well.

- Establishing shot (ES): sets the scene or shows the space of a scene; often a long shot or series of shots.

- Close-up (CS): the image being shot takes up at least 80 percent of the frame. There is also the extreme close-up that would show one part of the body or a portion of an object.

- Medium shot (MS): in-between LS and CS; people are seen from the waist up.

Focus

- Soft focus: when a director intentionally puts his or her object slightly out of focus to make the image look softer or unclear.

- Rack focus: when a director shifts the focus from one object to another in the same shot in order to direct the audience's attention.

- Deep focus: when the foreground and background are equally in focus.

Camera Angles

- Low angle (LA): camera shoots subject from below; has the effect of making the subject look larger than normal—strong, powerful, threatening.

- High angle (HA): camera is above the subject; usually has the effect of making the subject look smaller than normal—weak, powerless, trapped.

- Eye level (EL): accounts for 90 to 95 percent of the shots seen because it is most natural; camera is even with the key character's eyes.

- Dutch angle: shot that is tilted sideways on the horizontal line (also called "canted" angle); used to add tension to a static frame, it creates a sinister or distorted view of a character.

Sound

- Diegetic: sound that could be heard logically by the characters within the film; sound can also be internal diegetic, meaning that the sound can be heard only within the mind of one character.

- Nondiegetic: sound that could not be heard by characters; sound given directly to the audience by the director.

Lighting

- Low-key: scene is flooded with shadows and darkness; creates suspense/suspicion.
- High-key: scene is flooded with light; creates bright and open-looking scene.
- Neutral: neither bright nor dark—even lighting throughout the shot.
- Bottom/side: direct lighting from below or from one side; often dangerous or evil-looking, may convey split personality or moral ambiguity.
- Front/rear: soft, direct lighting on face or back of subject—may suggest innocence, create a "halo" effect.

Camera Movement

- Pan: stationary camera moves left or right.
- Tilt: stationary camera moves up or down.
- Zoom: the camera is stationary but the lens moves, making the objects appear to grow larger or smaller.
- Dolly: the camera itself is moving with the action—on a track, on wheels, or held by hand.

Editing Techniques

The most common is a "cut" to another image. Others are:

- Fade: scene fades to black or white; often implies that time has passed.
- Dissolve: an image fades into another; can create a connection between images.
- Crosscutting: cut to action that is happening simultaneously; also called parallel editing.
- Flashback: movement into action that has happened previously, often signified by a change in music, voice-over narration, or a dissolve; a "flash-forward" leads us ahead in time.
- Eye-line match: a shot of a person looking, then a cut to what he or she saw, followed by a cut back for a reaction.

Mise-en-Scène

This term refers to what appears within the frame of the shot, including decorations, props, acting, lighting, and makeup.

Appendix B: Blank Activity Charts

Film and Literature Analysis:
Prediction

Film/Novel	Predictions about Character, Theme, Setting	Reasons for Predictions

Film and Reading Strategies:
Responding to the Text

Film/Story/ Poem	I liked it when . . .	It reminded me of . . .	I felt confused when . . .

Film and Reading Strategies:
Levels of Questioning

TITLES	QUESTIONS
	Level One:
	Level Two:
	Level Three:
	Level One:
	Level Two:
	Level Three:
	Level One:
	Level Two:
	Level Three:

Film & Reading Strategies:
Storyboarding Activity # 1

What did you want   What lines helped
to demonstrate?   you see this?

SHOT #1

```
┌─────────────────────────┐
│                         │
│                         │
│                         │
│                         │
│                         │
└─────────────────────────┘
```

SHOT #2

```
┌─────────────────────────┐
│                         │
│                         │
│                         │
│                         │
│                         │
└─────────────────────────┘
```

SHOT #3

```
┌─────────────────────────┐
│                         │
│                         │
│                         │
│                         │
│                         │
└─────────────────────────┘
```

What music or sound effects would you imagine in this
scene? Why?

```
          Film & Reading Strategies:
            Storyboarding Activity # 2
```

Title_____   Director_____

Group_____   Chapter_____   Page #_____

Summary of Scene:

SHOT #

```
┌────────────────────┐    Intended Effect of Shot:
│                    │
│                    │
│                    │    Diegetic Sound:
│                    │
│                    │
│                    │    Nondiegetic Sound:
└────────────────────┘
```

Shot Type_____

Angle_____   **Lighting:**

Movement_____

Edit_____

SHOT #

```
┌────────────────────┐    Intended Effect of Shot:
│                    │
│                    │
│                    │    Diegetic Sound:
│                    │
│                    │
│                    │    Nondiegetic Sound:
└────────────────────┘
```

Shot Type_____

Angle_____   **Lighting:**

Movement_____

Edit_____

Film and Reading Strategies:
Soundtrack

Song Title	Where would it go in the story? Why?	What specific images do you imagine?

- Now, as the film's producer, you just found out that your budget allows for only *one* of the above songs. Which one would you choose and why?

- What other songs that you know of would fit in well with this story? Where would they fit?

Film and Literature Analysis:
Characterization

Considerations	Film: Character:	Novel/Story: Character:
Behavior		
Appearance		
Dialogue		
Feelings		
Director's/Writer's Craft		

Write a thesis statement about each of the characters:

    1.

    2.

Write a thesis statement of comparison between the two characters.

Film and Literature Analysis:
Setting

Considerations	Film:	Novel/Story:
Details of Setting		
Effect on Character(s)		
Director's/Writer's Craft		

Now, choose one of the settings above and, on the back of this sheet, draw a picture of the most important aspects of the setting.

Film and Literary Analysis:
Symbol Tally Sheet

As you watch each of the following film clips, keep track of the number of times that you see or hear a reference to the object that is acting as a symbol. Afterwards, identify the literal and make a guess about the possible metaphorical meanings of that symbol.

Film Title	Object	# of Visual References	# of Dialogue References	Literal Meaning	Metaphorical Meanings

Now, as we read the following short story, keep track of the references to the following that may be acting as symbols.

Story Title	Object	# of Direct References	# of Indirect References	Literal Meaning	Metaphorical Meanings

Film Viewing Notes:
Day #_____

TITLE: DIRECTOR:

STARS: YEAR:

SUMMARY: _____

_____

_____

_____

As you watch today's screening, jot down significant
observations for each of the following elements of the
film:

<u>THEATRICAL ELEMENTS</u>   <u>LITERARY ELEMENTS</u>
(costumes, props, sets, acting, etc.)   (conflicts, characterization,
                                                   setting, dialogue, etc.)

<u>CINEMATIC ELEMENTS</u>:
(shot type, angles, editing, sound, lighting, etc.)

<u>After Viewing</u>: Look back over your notes and explain the
intended effect of **<u>two</u>** or more of the cinematic, literary,
or theatrical elements you noticed. In other words, *why* did
the director choose to use them?

FREE WRITE: Write a paragraph or two of REFLECTION on today's
screening. What struck you most? What do you understand? What
questions do you have? Etc. Continue on back.

Your Name:

Note-Taking Form

Title: Director: Viewing Day:

Framing	Music
Jot down any places where you see a particularly interesting close-up or a long shot. Be sure to write down when it occurs.	Jot down any places where you hear a particularly interesting segment of music. Be sure to write down when it occurs.
Lighting	**Personal Response**
Jot down any places where you see a particularly interesting lighting choice. Be sure to write down when it occurs.	After you have finished watching today's segment, jot down what you think about what you saw. It can be what you liked/disliked, etc.

Take-home question:

Appendix C: Annotated List of Resources

There are so many books on film that you could spend years just looking through the stacks at your local bookstore. The following books are the ones that I have found to be the most helpful in learning about film and in beginning to use film in the classroom. I do not know of any texts on film that are designed to be read by high school students, but I have used several of the following books to prepare for class and even used several in class.

Books about Film in General

Bordwell, David, and Kristin Thompson. 2001. *Film Art: An Introduction.* 6th edition. New York: McGraw-Hill.

> Hands down, the single best film text I have used. It is extremely thorough, introducing the technical aspects of filmmaking and examining film in terms of its form, style, and history, as well as important critical theories. It includes hundreds of film stills, many in color, and, while it is designed for readers who are somewhat familiar with film, its many examples and easy writing style make it a great beginning text.

Dick, Bernard F. 1998. *Anatomy of Film.* 3rd edition. New York: St. Martin's Press.

> An even easier read than the Bordwell and Thompson text, this one covers much of the same ground, but it also breaks down many of the specific shot types and genres of film and discusses how to examine a film in its entirety. He includes a wonderful section on film subtexts and some interesting ideas on film and literature. When I need to try to understand some of the complex writings by various film theorists, I often open this book's section on film criticism; he synthesizes extremely well.

Ebert, Roger, ed. 1996. *Roger Ebert's Book of Film.* New York: W. W. Norton.

> Movie critic Ebert collected some of the best writing about film, acting, Hollywood, directing, and the love of the movies in this seven hundred page volume. Many great directors, actors, and producers talk openly about their craft. It is easy and very enjoyable to read.

Giannetti, Louis. 1999. *Understanding Movies*. 8th edition. Upper Saddle River, NJ: Prentice Hall.

> The fifth edition of this book was my very first film textbook, and now, in its eighth edition, it boasts color stills, and Leonardo DiCaprio on the cover. While it covers much of the same ground as the first two, it includes a sample storyboard for the cornfield sequence from *North by Northwest*, which I discussed in the section on film terminology. In addition to the film stills, Giannetti includes some of the best captions for those stills I have ever read in any book on any subject. You could learn just about everything you need to know just from reading those captions. Go ahead and read the rest though—it's very straightforward and clear.

Monaco, James. 1981. *How to Read a Film: The Art, Technology, Language, History, and Theory of Film and Media*. Rev. ed. New York: Oxford University Press.

> Wow. If you think the title is long, just wait until you see the book. When you have read this text—and understood it—you have reached the grail of film theory, and you're way out of my league. It includes, however, information absolutely essential to the study of film. Monaco is extremely well versed in the technology of cinema and in the signs and syntax of the language of film. There are a few stills, but even more significant are the many charts and diagrams. It may not be the place to start with film, but you'll be in great shape if you end up here.

Books about Film in the Classroom

Costanzo, William V. 1992. *Reading the Movies: Twelve Great Films on Video and How to Teach Them*. Urbana, IL: NCTE.

> Don't be misled by the title, this book does much more than help us teach twelve films; the first half of it synthesizes a lot of the information contained in a number of the excellent books on film study, including the texts listed above, but Costanzo does it specifically for English teachers, not for film scholars. The second half is where he gives a brief analysis of the suggested films, along with great resources and suggested activities. The material is geared toward high school and college students, and some of the applications would be useful with middle school students as well.

Teasley, Alan B., and Ann Wilder. 1997. *Reel Conversations: Reading Films with Young Adults*. Portsmouth, NH: Heinemann.

> I had been using film in my classroom for some time when this book was given to me by a district supervisor, and it changed my

thinking in many ways. First, the authors reminded me that film is about more than just the cinematic techniques that a director uses. To forget about the theatrical and literary aspects, which I had done, is to lose sight of much of a film's power to affect its audience. The authors also include some great ways to teach film genre to students, which obviously has many parallels to teaching literature. And last, they did a great deal of legwork for us by putting together lists of possible films in just about every conceivable category. This is a very readable book and a wonderful resource.

Books about Filmmaking

In the same way that reading books about the craft of writing can offer insight into the analysis of literature, reading books designed for the beginning film director has taught me a tremendous amount about film theory and practice.

Cantine, John, Susan Howard, and Brady Lewis. 1995. *Shot By Shot: A Practical Guide to Filmmaking.* 2nd edition. Pittsburgh: Pittsburgh Filmmakers.

> A pocket-sized guide to the lenses, film stock, and lighting information that directors need, this text also contains worthwhile information on editing, sound, and shot composition.

Harmon, Renee. 1993. *The Beginning Filmmaker's Guide to Directing.* New York: Walker.

> After reading this book, I defy you not to be tempted to pick up a video camera and start shooting the next great Oscar winner. It is very easy to read and understand. In addition to using Harmon's very helpful charts on camera placement and lighting, I have also taken some of her ideas about screenwriting and film budgets to support a culminating film project that my students do.

Pincus, Edward, and Steven Ascher. 1999. *The Filmmaker's Handbook: A Comprehensive Guide for the Digital Age.* New York: Plume.

> Way more than probably your average filmmaker needs to know about filmmaking, so it's barely on our radar charts, but I have learned a lot about the technology behind the movies from this book. For our purposes, it contains a worthwhile section on sound recording and an interesting description of how various lenses can create different perspectives on film to create subjective shots

Resources on Media Literacy

In addition to resources that focus on film, filmmaking, or classroom uses of film, teachers may find it useful to explore the following organizations that promote and support media literacy education.

Center for Media Literacy (www.medialit.org)

> This organization's Web site describes the group as "dedicated to a new vision of literacy for the 21st century: the ability to communicate competently in all media forms, print and electronic, as well as to access, understand, analyze and evaluate the powerful images, words and sounds that make up our contemporary mass media culture. Our mission is to bring media literacy education to every child, every school and every home in North America."

Alliance for a Media Literate America (www.amlainfo.org)

> With founding members including the Center for Media Literacy, this group works to bring together "a diverse alliance of individuals and organizations to create a national non-profit membership organization that will be a key force in bringing media literacy education to all 60 million students in the United States, their parents, their teachers, and others who care about youth." This professional development collaborative organizes and hosts the annual National Media Education Conference for teachers, administrators, and community leaders.

Appendix D: Index of Films Discussed

Title	Director	Rating	Activity	Page
Apocalypse Now	Francis Ford Coppola	R	Terminology	33
Blue Velvet	David Lynch	R	Irony	90
Bride of Frankenstein	James Whale	Not rated	Complete film	123
A Christmas Story	Bob (Benjamin) Clark	PG	Responding, point of view	44, 81
Citizen Kane	Orson Welles	Not rated	Predicting, irony	37, 91
The Color Purple	Steven Spielberg	PG-13	Questioning	51
The Conversation	Francis Ford Coppola	PG	Responding	46
Crooklyn	Spike Lee	PG-13	Complete film	106
Cyrano de Bergerac	Jean-Paul Rappeneau	PG	Complete film	143
Edward Scissorhands	Tim Burton	PG-13	Irony	92
Elizabeth	Shekhar Kapur	R	Characterization, complete film	61, 148
E.T. the Extra-Terrestrial	Steven Spielberg	PG	Complete film	102
Falling Down	Joel Schumacher	R	Setting	68
Frankenstein	James Whale	Not rated	Complete film	123
Ghost	Jerry Zucker	PG-13	Predicting	39
Good Morning, Vietnam	Barry Levinson	R	Irony	89
Groundhog Day	Harold Ramis	PG	Responding	44
Henry V	Kenneth Branagh	Not rated	Responding, characterization	45, 64
Jaws	Steven Spielberg	PG	Point of view	79
King of the Hill	Steven Soderbergh	PG-13	Complete film	113
Life Is Beautiful	Roberto Benigni	PG-13	Complete film	117
The Lion King	Roger Allers and Rob Minkoff	G	Complete film	98
The Man Who Shot Liberty Valance	John Ford	Not rated	Symbol	86
North by Northwest	Alfred Hitchcock	Not rated	Terminology	29
Notorious	Alfred Hitchcock	Not rated	Point of view	74
Othello	Orson Welles	Not rated	Terminology	26
Philadelphia	Jonathon Demme	PG-13	Terminology	30

continued on next page

Title	Director	Rating	Activity	Page
The Piano	Jane Campion	R	Symbol	87
Psycho	Alfred Hitchcock	Not rated	Point of view, symbol	80, 84
Rear Window	Alfred Hitchcock	Not rated	Predicting	37
The Remains of the Day	James Ivory	PG	Characterization	63
Rocky	John Avildsen	PG	Complete film	132
Smoke Signals	Chris Eyre	PG-13	Questioning, complete film	50, 139
Sunset Boulevard	Billy Wilder	Not rated	Setting	69
Titanic	James Cameron	PG-13	Questioning	48
Vertigo	Alfred Hitchcock	Not rated	Setting	70

Author

Photo by Ariela Edelman

Photo by Ariela Edelman

John Golden has taught English at public and private high schools in Virginia and Maryland and currently teaches at Grant High School in Portland, Oregon. He has presented strategies for using film in the classroom for hundreds of teachers around the country. He specifically selected the low-angle close-up with side lighting for one of his author's pictures; to know what else he is saying about himself, be sure to read Chapter 1.

This book was typeset in Palatino and Helvetica by Electronic Imaging.
The typefaces used on the cover were Insignia and Au Casablanca.
The book was printed on 60-lb. Finch Opaque by IPC Communication Services.